T0078420

SEXUALITY & HOLINESS.

Remaining loving and biblically-grounded in a rapidly shifting culture

MIKE WILLIAMS

WESTBOW
PRESS®
A DIVISION OF THOMAS NELSON
& ZONDERVAN

WestBow Press books may be ordered through booksellers or by contacting:

WestBow Press
A Division of Thomas Nelson & Zondervan
1663 Liberty Drive
Bloomington, IN 47403
www.westbowpress.com
844-714-3454

ISBN: 978-1-6642-6969-9 (sc)
ISBN: 978-1-6642-6970-5 (hc)
ISBN: 978-1-6642-6968-2 (e)

Library of Congress Control Number: 2022911354

Print information available on the last page.

WestBow Press rev. date: 8/3/2022

I know Mike Williams to be a man of integrity and he has approached this important subject with humility and compassion. I would encourage you to bear this in mind as you read this book which focuses on the biblical basis of sexuality, gender and relationships.

The foundation of this book is the Bible which is considered to be the infallible Word of God and therefore completely relevant even in these turbulent days.

Throughout the book the emphasis is that God is good and rather than being a killjoy, He is actually the author of joy who longs to bless people. May this book replace confusion with clarity and help people to realise that the biblical basis for sexual relationships and gender is best for all.

Reverend John Bridger

A balanced view is often challenging to maintain but greatly appreciated. This is certainly true when it comes to Christians addressing the rapidly changing topic of the LGBTQ+ community.

A balanced view that is willing to join the conversation, listen to others with different views and then carefully articulate our Heavenly Father's statements on the topic as found in His Word... this is challenging indeed. However, if you would greatly appreciate such a view, you are holding the right book in your hands, *Sexuality & Holiness* by Pastor Mike Williams.

Elbert Smith, Ph.D.

In a world of cultural shifts, we are all searching for truth, direction for our purpose and guidance as to how we can live our lives to the full. As someone working with young people who are engulfed with pressing ethical topics of sexuality, gender and relationships, I have found this book to be an incredible resource which has challenged and encouraged me greatly. I highly recommend it for its honest tone and accessible style to leaders and members of youth groups alike.

Mike has done a great job in speaking the truth with love and clarity, pointing us in the right direction, straight to God's Word.

Jenny Ogwal, Youth Leader

John Knox the famous Scottish reformer was once asked by Queen Mary: "Who am I to believe? You and your followers teach one thing while many church leaders teach another." Knox replied, "Your Majesty, you should not rely on the teachings of men. Instead, you should only believe and trust in what is plainly and clearly taught in the Word of God."

This resource highlights what the Word of God plainly teaches about gender and sexuality. If you want to obey what Scripture teaches rather than follow the views of various church leaders, then I cannot recommend this book too highly.

I would love to see faithful Christians present a copy of *Sexuality & Holiness* to every pastor and church leader throughout the country. Written in an easy-to-read style, rather than in the form of a dry theological treatise, this resource is ideal for sharing with others, so that they too can learn that the Living God really does have something very clearly to say.

Pastor John of Strengthen the Faithful, author of internetpulpit. co.uk

This book is dedicated to my beautiful wife Rachel, who supports me in ministry and is the most wonderful and creative mum to our three precious children.

Contents

Foreword

A balanced view is often challenging to maintain but greatly appreciated. This is certainly true when it comes to Christians addressing the rapidly changing topic of the LGBTQ+ community.

It is easy to find Christians who align themselves with the latest cultural positions, perhaps in a desire to be relevant to contemporary culture or perhaps to avoid the intense opposition to all dissenting voices. Secondly, it is also easy to find Christians who hold to traditional or biblical values without even listening to current conversation. Furthermore, it is easy to find Christians who attempt to ignore the discussion altogether.

A balanced view that is willing to join the conversation, listen to others with different views and then carefully articulate our heavenly Father's statements on the topic as found in His Word... this is challenging indeed. However, if you would greatly appreciate such a view, you are holding the right book in your hands, *Sexuality & Holiness* by Pastor Mike Williams.

You are about to eavesdrop on some of Mike's conversations and thoughts which make very clear he is not inherently opposed to the LGBTQ+ community. He writes, 'I, for one, would be delighted to endorse same-sex marriage, were it affirmed by God's Word, the Bible.' Mike is certainly not included among those who are unwilling to listen or join the conversation. But Mike continues the previous quote, 'However, here in lies one of the greatest questions of our times... *Is* it affirmed by the Bible?' For those like Mike and me who have found that, as Jesus said, God's 'word is truth' (John 17:17) and it guides to a life of true freedom, that becomes the fundamental question.

You are about to find yourself in the middle of the challenge that comes from attempting to obey the second most important commandment of all, again according to Jesus, 'You shall love your neighbour as yourself' (Matthew 22:39), while remembering that God's plan is the highest good for every one of His creations. We never live our lives contrary to His plan without harming ourselves.

Additionally, Mike wisely examines the LGBTQ+ movement as something beyond the community itself. He encourages us to put on spiritual antennae and question whether there is more going on here, than first meets the eye.

Although being willing to enter the conversation while maintaining a biblical view can seem exhausting, Mike is not going to leave you in limbo. He concludes with very practical steps as to how any church, or you as a reader, can move forward. Even if you may not hold to every application of how God intervenes, Mike concludes with an outline for moving forward that seems both insightful and helpful.

In January of this year, my wife Kay and I lived in Surrey and were members of Pastor Mike's congregation where I had the privilege of serving alongside the elders. We have since accepted a position in the States, however during our time in Surrey we sat under Mike's teaching and watched him beautifully live out his teaching in his role as pastor and in his personal life. This book reflects the balance of his life:

an exemplary desire to love God and His word while loving his neighbours. Prepare to be challenged by this balanced approach to such an important topic in our day, *Sexuality & Holiness*.

Elbert Smith, Ph.D., April 2022

Thank you...

I'd like to thank some very special people who made it possible for this book to come together. Firstly, I'd like to thank Katharine Grimes for being willing to give up countless hours in editing this book, and her husband Paul and family for being willing to support her in this.

Likewise, I'd like to thank my good friend, Pastor Barry Mortlock, who sat through all the editing meetings to ensure Katharine and I were not alone in this project. This, we believe, is essential for all Christians, as we seek to be above reproach, to honour our spouses and, most of all, to honour our Lord.

A very special thank you goes to my wife Rachel who always encourages me and is the perfect wife to me. I am incredibly thankful to God for you, and our precious children.

Finally, and not exhaustively, the prayer network who prayed for us throughout as we prayerfully considered the book and what should be included. You know who you are!

You are all very much loved and appreciated, thank you!

Introduction

The kitchen in our family home resembles Clapham Junction. So much passes through it from every family member, our two cats, countless bags of washing, drying and ironing… and, most importantly, discussions and debates.

My wife Rachel has her own mind, which is what I love about her. So, when I ask Rachel her opinion, I can be assured I will get an honest response, making her the very best person to share my heart with.

On this occasion, I told Rachel that I have a burden on my heart.

I told her that I've noticed a huge increase in activity around gender and sexuality over the past few years – and it's making me feel like I want to press the pause button and say, *"Whoa, what's going on here and why?"*

Currently, there is such a major push everywhere by and on behalf of the LGBTQ+ community.

It feels like people are falling over backwards to be seen to be championing this movement.

What began as an equality movement for civil partnerships some years ago, has now morphed into something that is visible in nearly every area of our modern society and leaving a firm footprint. This movement is reshaping films and television by the inclusion of homosexual, bisexual, trans and non-binary characters such as Superman who will feature in future comics as a bisexual man; it is encouraging sports stars to wear rainbow armbands and laces in honour of LGBTQ+; Pride marches in the name of LGBTQ+ are taking place all over the world; businesses must now show proactive and public support of LGBTQ+ or face being frowned upon and slandered on social media; and even schools are repeatedly teaching our children they can be whoever or whatever they want to be and marry people of whatever gender they wish to when they are older. It is no longer unusual for families to have same-sex parents and it is hard to ignore the 'he/she/they/their/them' pronouns preference that seems like the latest politically correct campaign of the hour.

Everything seems to be moving so quickly and it makes me want to ask several key questions...

- How do we know if this movement pleases God and whether we, as His people, the Church, can embrace it?
- Is the prevalence of LGBTQ+ in our societies symptomatic of a wider underlying issue; that humanity has turned it back on God's standard of holiness and sought to create its own brand of morality?
- Where are the prophets of our day: those church pastors who are willing to speak up for God's truth in our days, regardless of the damage it may do to their reputation and popularity?

John the Baptist had a clear message of repentance to a sinful world, one that eventually lifted off his head! Even so, he had no hesitation in delivering it.

I told Rachel all this (including all my questions) and she listened patiently. A good thing, as I had a lot to say!

I finished by telling her, in the face of all this emphasis placed upon LGBTQ+, I'm unsure how to respond as a man seeking to honour God above all.

On the one hand, I feel like the increasingly pushy, no right of reply, 'you'd better affirm it' strategy imposed on everyone, makes me question whether, in fact, there is a darker spiritual agenda behind it. Certainly, the degree of confusion and division that people are experiencing in it all (always hallmarks of the enemy's involvement) makes me recollect the words of Ephesians 6:12 (NIV):

> For our struggle is not against flesh and blood, but
> against the rulers, against the authorities, against
> the powers of this dark world and against the
> spiritual forces of evil in the heavenly realms.

On the other hand, I told Rachel that I'm acutely aware this issue is a really tricky one to tackle without bringing prejudice into the mix.

Of course, I must acknowledge that in writing on this subject I bring my own background and bias into the picture as a white, heterosexual man who has been raised in a western society.

That said, I don't want to be one of those whacky pastors who preaches harshly against anything that smacks in the face of traditional views.

I don't want to be unfair or intentionally, to hurt anyone.

That is not my agenda.

But I do want to be open to any change that God might be bringing to His Church in how we approach issues of same-sex relationships, sexuality and gender identity today.

What's more, I do feel the speed and apparent aggressiveness of this movement is concerning; it seems like it has the capacity to grow beyond the point of return and that unless churches embrace it, persecution could be around the corner.

I continued by saying, "Rachel, I believe this may even be a sign that we are closer to the end than we think."

Now, don't get me wrong, I don't have a date and it could be a long way off, but I believe we may be entering a period of increased intensity of the birth pains Jesus spoke about in Matthew 24. Rachel often reminds me that in labour, the closer together the contractions and the more painful they get, the closer the arrival of the baby. Could the increasing volume of global issues (climate change, wars, famines, natural disasters, and disease to name a few...) and growing godlessness in our world today be telling us something about *our* times?

Are we getting closer to the arrival?

Not of the baby King but of the conquering King?

(Obviously, this was a little more dramatic than our usual dinner table conversations! Nonetheless, I had her attention on this occasion.)

I ended by saying, "I am going to pray for some sort of confirmation, as I really don't want to be off on a nutty agenda."

Rachel smiled at me, and that was that... at least, for that evening.

The next day, I went to the local school to drop off my children. As I stood in the playground, a member of our church came up to me who had not attended for nearly two years, since the outbreak of Covid-19. She said, "Mike, I had a dream about you last night. In the dream I sensed you have been given a revelation about a time, and you are right."

There was another Christian friend there with me who witnessed the conversation, and he was as puzzled as I was. However, later that day I remembered my discussion with Rachel and my prayer. I had asked God for confirmation that my uneasiness had been put there by Him and that what is happening in our day with the prevalence of the LGBTQ+ movement is a sign of the gear change towards the End Times! Could this dream be an indication I was on the right track in seeking to obey and follow God's leading?

I want to be very clear and say I am not taking this dream as an absolute confirmation; I am aware we will never know the time or the date of the End when Jesus promises to return, but I believe we must be alert and awake and understand the times we are in *right now* (see Matthew 16).

The world is changing...

There are protests weekly,

growing disrespect for leaders sadly lacking in integrity,

Brexit,

wars in many places all the time,

climate change pointing to how human sin is destroying the planet...

And of course, in recent years, the advent of Covid-19!

Amongst it all, there is the civil unrest of racial injustice, the moral decline of abortion, and the subject of this book: the ever-increasing sexuality and gender debate that will no doubt cause much division in the coming days from within and without the worldwide Church.

As I write, some denominations have already decided to embrace same-sex marriage; others are considering it on the basis of dwindling numbers. But when were numbers ever a reason to review doctrine?[1]

What a desperately difficult discussion this has become!

Why?

Because, if we are honest, unless we are prejudiced, why wouldn't we want two consenting adults of the same sex who love each other to be happily married?

I, for one, would be delighted to endorse same-sex marriage, were it affirmed by God's Word, the Bible. However, here in lies one of the greatest questions of our times...

Is it affirmed by the Bible?

Are same-sex relationships sinful in God's eyes?

Have we lost the fear of God in our approach to culture?

And if so, more importantly, what are we going to do about it?

I also have a conviction in my heart to address the other elephant in the room...

If a pastor, or a Christian generally, for that matter, decides that they cannot affirm homosexual relationships, is it fair to call them a homophobe?

These are the reasons behind writing this book; my hope and prayer is that it will help the reader understand why as believers our approach towards the LGBTQ+ movement and community is such an important topic of the day and what the

Bible has to say to us about it. I hope it may help those with a different understanding to my own to see the reasoning behind my position and that it is not because I am prejudiced against LGBTQ+.

I also want to enable Christians who share my view to be confident in why they do, and to encourage pastors to stand and teach on this topic with integrity whilst ensuring we practise love towards all people regardless of sexuality.

In the first part of this book, I'll set the scene by explaining my own story in terms of engaging with LGBTQ+ and then unpacking why the Bible can be trusted as an infallible source and how we can define sin.

Then, I'll explore what the Bible actually teaches on same-sex relationships in the Old and the New Testament. Finally, I'll tackle how each of us can be alert to the changing times around us; taking up the challenge to be discerning and faithful in holding fast to what the Bible says alongside demonstrating Jesus' unconditional love to everyone around us.

There are multiple opinions on LGBTQ+ floating around the worldwide Church at present, but what would it look like for us to read what the Bible says, understand and take it seriously, and ultimately, see sexuality and holiness *through God's eyes*?

Mike Williams – January 2022

PART 1

SETTING THE SCENE

1

No right of reply

MY STORY

I became a pastor in training in 2009.

I was never academic, but my story is about God doing the unexpected; leading me from a nine-year career in commercial banking to gaining a degree in Applied Theology and taking on my first church as Senior Pastor at the age of 31.

I took over from a pastor who planted the church twenty-two years earlier. With no experience at all, you could say that taking over this church of roughly 275 people, gave me some very BIG boots to fill. That said, after turning down the role several times, I had an encounter with God in a little chapel in Ffald y Brenin, Wales, which changed my life forever. Following it, I made the decision to take up the post of Senior Pastor, and the church has continued to grow today, by the grace of God.

Why am I telling you this?

Well, firstly, when I stood in front of several hundreds of people for my ordination at the church, I was asked why I felt called to become a pastor.

My response was: "I have encountered Jesus, I have responded to His call and, having come from a largely atheist family put off by pastors that have done terrible things over the years, I believe I am being called to do it the right way, God's way... I want to restore people's confidence in God – people like my father who does not trust the Church, and, in particular, does not trust its ministers."

On the day of my ordination, I felt strongly that there was a need for Spirit-filled pastors in the Church; pastors who have a conviction to preach and teach God's Word, and an equally strong conviction to live it out!

Today, I still believe this.

I believe we need to be *Nehemiahs* of our time.

When Nehemiah set out to rebuild the walls of Jerusalem, he was motivated not only by the deep conviction of his heart, but by a desire to act wisely in everything. He consistently held a tool in one hand and a weapon in the other as he faced huge opposition from others who sought to discourage him and stamp out the vision to rebuild the walls (see Nehemiah chapter 4).

Today, we need to do the same; we need to assess the Church and to rebuild its walls so that God is the foundation, recognising that we may well face opposition, and even attack.

The weapon of choice for every believer in the twenty-first century can be none other than the Word of God, handled prayerfully:

For the Word of God is alive and active. Sharper than any double edged sword, it penetrates even to dividing soul and spirit, joints and marrow; it judges the thoughts and attitudes of the heart.

(Hebrews 4:12, NIV)

As a priesthood of believers, we must preach the whole counsel of God's Word even when it hurts, we must be willing to be rejected on account of Jesus' name and God's instruction, as Jesus promised we would be:

Everyone will hate you because of me, but the one who stands firm to the end will be saved.

(Mark 13:13, NIV)

All this formed a conviction in my heart which has stayed with me to this day, challenging me to keep going back to God's Word, no matter the cultural shifts around us.

That said, I wish to be completely clear:

It does not mean I wish to remove love from the equation.

So, it was with this dual focus in my heart that I approached the next part of my training to become a pastor.

Prior to my ordination, I trained at a brilliant college called Moorlands in Dorset, where I gained a degree in Applied Theology. Afterwards, I was informed I would have to study for a further four years at a denominational college in order to be accredited as a pastor.[2]

At this time, I was asked to complete several papers, one of which was on a subject of my choice. I chose to write a paper entitled 'Is homosexuality a sin?'. As, let's face it, the answer to that question is important to all pastors, like it or not.

3

If liberal pastors are wrong, that's a lot of people who have been given false hope.

If, however, conservative pastors are wrong, that means big numbers of people repelled by a seemingly legalistic and loveless Church.

Either way, it's important to ask the question...

More than once, I have heard it said in a pastors' gathering: "I'm not concerned about gay marriage, it's not a salvation issue."

But can we be sure of that?

Surely, to receive God's saving grace, we must be willing to accept all sin and to turn from it.

So, does that work if we enter into a faith relationship with God saying, "Sorry God, but you're wrong on the sexuality stuff... It's not actually a sin in the twenty-first century."

This is why I chose the subject of homosexuality for my paper, and having researched, read the Bible, and prayed, I submitted it.

After some time, I received the critique of my paper.

I was told that it was clear I was 'a conservative evangelical' and was advised to write 'an addendum assessing more liberal theologians'. There was a tone to this response that jarred with me, and I couldn't help feeling that I didn't see myself in this light. I simply read the Bible and used many biblical references in my paper.

But this was not all.

The assessor went on to ask a further question with words to this effect: if I believed the Old Testament law of Leviticus 20:13 (as a revelation about how God felt about relationships outside of a male and a female) was relevant and applicable today, did I think that Christians should in fact, *stone* homosexual people?

What a question!

Of course, these words greatly hurt me, as my heart is to see every human being draw near to God and receive His free gift of eternal salvation.

I went on to write the addendum.

I assessed the very perspectives and more of the theologians and scholars whom the assessor had recommended. The paper was easy to write, as the theological views in the recommended books were based lightly on Scripture and largely on cultural shifts.

I submitted the addendum and awaited the response.

But that response did not come.

In fact, I chased it several times for several months until finally, I was informed that the paper had been passed on to the Principal of the College, for him to mark. Something in me told me this was not because they wanted to publish it. So, I chased the paper for several more months without response until, eventually, I informed the leaders of the denomination that I would like to rescind my application to be an accredited minister, as my views were obviously not what they were looking for.

Just one week later, I received a response from them saying I had passed – with no further explanation.

All this served to highlight for me that division in the Church regarding the LGBTQ+ movement is increasing, and it is not clear who stands where on the liberal versus conservative spectrum. We cannot make any assumptions about individual denominations or individual colleges although one thing is certain: Liberal churches and the views held by society are on course for a head on collision with those churches who hold a more conservative view.

It doesn't end there, however.

Prior to writing my paper, I was invited to a Ministerial Selection Committee.

As part of this process, I was placed in a room with six trainee ministers and told that we would be given a question to discuss together, whilst being assessed by an external interviewer.

Can you believe it? The question we were asked was: 'Will you baptise a homosexual person in an actively gay lifestyle and welcome them into membership within your church?'

One very strong-willed woman in the group instantly piped up with, "I will not only do it, but I will be pushing to marry the homosexual community too, as soon as I'm ordained." Then, three other trainee ministers all followed with loud voices... They all agreed with the woman who was for gay marriage. That only left myself and a Pentecostal minister, and I am pleased to say my Pentecostal friend didn't let me down. He proceeded to explain why he couldn't agree with the other ministers, citing a few biblical reasons, for which he was strongly shot down.

That left only me to respond...

I stood up and proceeded to talk about the importance of repentance and turning from sin before entering the baptismal waters, explaining that, in fact, I believed the question should be, 'Is homosexuality a sin?'

Then, I sat down.

The room was a bit quiet initially and I distinctly remember that for the remainder of the assessment, it felt as if I had said something outrageous.

Had I?

Is it important where we as individuals stand on this particular issue?

At its heart, is this about merely loving people and fully accepting all forms of relationship... or is there a deeper, spiritual issue caught up within it that we need to consider?

My experiences during my accreditation seemed to demonstrate that currently, the way the Church responds to LGBTQ+, is undefined and can produce a very messy, confusing, highly charged and divisive debate.

Like I said before, isn't it time to press the pause button? To ask the question: "*Whoa, what's going on here and why?*"

To cap it all off, my thoughts on this were reinforced by recent events.

I was on our annual family holiday with my in-laws.

Several conversations on the subject of homosexuality came up with my brothers-in-law, both of whom I get on well with and it was interesting to see the variety of views expressed. While one was passionate in stating that the Church needs to move with the times, the other said he did not care about the Church at this stage in his life but is pro 'love is love' – regardless of whether it be heterosexual or homosexual. As for my own opinion, I referred to the Bible and shared how I believe our expression of sexuality becomes a kingdom-decision (something we will consider further in subsequent chapters). However, despite the polite discussion, one of my brothers-in-law referred to me as the 'homophobic pastor,' more than once.

Whether or not he really believes this, I do not know. But the reality is, unless a pastor embraces homosexuality, often society and parts of the Church brand them with this new 'homophobic' identity.

In all my conversations, the sad truth is, unless you embrace it, there is often never *a right of reply*!

CHOOSING TO STAND

In light of this, I believe it is time for pastors and ministers like myself to stand on our conviction concerning this matter through the reading of Scripture and a healthy fear of God, which Proverbs 9:10 tells us is, 'the beginning of [all] wisdom' (NIV).

There is a loud voice in favour of the Church embracing the LGBTQ+ movement and the changes it will mean for church doctrine, but there seems to be an intermittent whisper from those who wish to uphold the Word of God correctly.

But please don't mistake me.

I am not looking to be loveless in my explanation of Scripture.

I serve a God whose Word is infallible but is the very source of love and I wish my views on every aspect of life to mirror His approach.

Just as Nehemiah simultaneously held up a tool and a weapon in his hands to rebuild the walls, I believe today, we are called to hold up love and biblical truth in tandem.

I have met so many wonderful people who would class themselves part of the LGBTQ+ community and have found each individual to be very endearing. I've enjoyed getting to know each one and hear their unique stories.

If that is you, reader, please know that I'm always ready to hear those stories. I recognise it must feel like there is a disjoint between what the Church is saying when they say that they 'love' you, yet simultaneously expect you to change your behaviour and reconsider your lifestyle choices.

You have a right to tell your story and to be real about its highs and lows.

And just so, I ask that you respect my desire to share *my* thoughts; that there might be a right of reply and that I might choose to point to what the Bible says.

Love regardless

LOVELESS CHURCH?

I recently visited a good friend of mine who happens to be a lecturer in a theology college. Whilst our main reason for meeting was friendship and to discuss a mission trip, the subject of LGBTQ+ and the Church also came up during our conversation.

What my friend told me will never leave me.

My friend spoke of a visit to Ukraine some years ago, and how during this visit he got caught up in a shocking and violent protest.

He and his colleagues were sitting in a town square when a hoard of angry protestors came in their thousands with awful, aggressive placards against the LGBTQ+ community who were holding some sort of Pride march that same day.

My Christian friend was petrified, along with the LGBTQ+ folk gathered, as this protest threatened to get very nasty.

However, my friend was also very angry... not only because of this terrible treatment of the LGBTQ+ community, but because of who was also represented in the protesting crowd. He told me he was horrified to see that the protest was being led by some sort of national front. Yet, it wasn't the national front that shocked him, it was who he realised had teamed up with them... the Orthodox Church!

The Church!

My friend said that this encounter angered and hurt him so much, that he promised himself he would never speak against the LGBTQ+ community.

THE GREATEST COMMANDMENT

This is the danger of discussing this very relevant and very delicate issue.

On the one hand, we must ensure that we handle the Word of God correctly and live it out in our day-to-day lives as doers, not just hearers, of the Word.

At the same time, we must remember the great commands which Jesus emphasised in Matthew 22:36-40 (NIV):

> *Teacher, which is the greatest commandment in the Law? Jesus replied: "'Love the Lord your God with all your heart and with all your soul and with all your mind. This is the first and greatest commandment. And the second is like it: 'Love your neighbour as yourself. All the Law and the Prophets hang on these two commandments.'"*

Is this passage not sobering when looking at the topic of this book?

It's likely we all know Christian believers who get on their high horse when it comes to topics like the LGBTQ+ debate – in fact, at times, I'll admit that I have been one of them. Some may seem more dogmatic and aggressive than others, but I cannot deny having become impassioned, myself, on occasion. However, we must all remind ourselves that where human beings are involved, the only foundation to every discussion can be love.

These are the greatest commands God has given us:

Love God.

Love your neighbour.

In fact, Jesus even taught us to love our enemies.

> *But to you who are listening I say: Love your enemies, do good to those who hate you, bless those who curse you, pray for those who mistreat you.*

(Luke 6:27-28, NIV)

So, if this is the kind of love that Jesus encourages, shouldn't we as His followers, the Church, extend that same love towards all individuals, including those who comprise the LGBTQ+ community. Certainly, they are not *our* enemy.

Surely, it is possible to love people even if you don't affirm their chosen lifestyle?

That is why before we consider what the Bible says on the topic of LGBTQ+, I want to remind us that we cannot begin to grapple with it unless we have first grappled with the importance of loving all people on every side of this debate.

In fact, we must remember the words of the apostle Paul in 1 Corinthians 13:1-4 (NIV):

> *If I speak in the tongues of men or of angels, but do not have love, I am only a resounding gong or a clanging cymbal.*

If I have the gift of prophecy and can fathom all mysteries and all knowledge, and if I have a faith that can move mountains, but do not have love, I am nothing. If I give all I possess to the poor and give over my body to hardship that I may boast, but do not have love, I gain nothing.

Further on in verse 13, Paul says: 'And now these three remain: faith, hope and love. But the greatest of these is love.'

Now, I know the context of this passage is focused on the Church concerning spiritual gifts. But that does not give grounds for us to overlook love as a characteristic central to being a Christian. In all we are and do, the people we encounter must be able to see that there is something different about us.

That no matter the biblical knowledge we may possess, it means nothing if we do not first show *authentic Christlike love* to everyone around us.

LOVE LISTENS

We must recognise also that for many who would class themselves as part of the LGBTQ+ community, they would say they were born the way they are and that their sexuality is part of their identity.

Now, I would question whether our sexuality really can be our identity; after all, how many heterosexuals would class their sexual preference for members of the opposite gender, as their identity? However, when it comes to being born with our sexual orientation, it would seem possible and fair that this is true. (Sexual orientation as opposed to sexual preference is something I will explore further in subsequent chapters.) For many without faith, in their words, it is just the way nature has formed them.

In contrast, a more conservative believer would say that according to the Bible, God made us 'male and female,' yet we were corrupted by the Fall (see Genesis 3). They would go on to say that one major consequence of the Fall is the corruption of humanity's original blueprint – which could include our sexual orientation.

Psalm 51:1-6 supports this by declaring we are sinful, even in the womb:

> Have mercy on me, O God,
> according to your unfailing love;
> according to your great compassion
> blot out my transgressions.
> Wash away all my iniquity
> and cleanse me from my sin.
> For I know my transgressions,
> and my sin is always before me.
> Against you, you only, have I sinned
> and done what is evil in your sight;
> so you are right in your verdict
> and justified when you judge.
> **Surely I was sinful at birth,**
> **sinful from the time my mother conceived me.**
> Yet you desired faithfulness even in the womb;
> you taught me wisdom in that secret place.

(NIV, my emphasis added)

If it is true that some are born with the feeling that they are born in the wrong body, or they experience same-sex attraction, it is vital we treat them with absolute compassion.

That said, we need to consider both sides of the coin: Considering the focus placed in our schools today on affirming 'coming out' or declaring oneself to be non-binary or transgender, it could also be argued that there is scope for children and young people to become increasingly confused with their own and others' sexuality preferences.

No matter our perceptions, the important thing is that compassion and love are always central when sharing the true gospel of repentance with those of the LGBTQ+ community.

I shall never forget the module I studied on Christian witness to Muslims whilst training to be a pastor. During it, something the lecturer said especially grabbed my attention: "How do you get a Muslim to slam the door in your face? Tell them Jesus is the Son of God!"

Now, pause for a moment.

It's likely that many of us will be thinking, "Yeah, well, it's true and they need to hear it!"

Yet, what is more useful in the mission of God? A truth spoken in ten seconds and a door slammed in your face? Or a slowly built friendship whereby a Christian and Muslim can share mutually about their experiences of Jesus?

It's love, combined with respect for the person we are trying to reach, which helps leave the door open to conversations; conversations that could in time lead to the cross... and this truth applies to the LGBTQ+ community. Can we be respectful and loving enough to keep the door open to conversation – even if we hold a different view?

GOD WORKS IN MYSTERIOUS WAYS

I preached a sermon series, some months ago, called: 'Candid Jesus – the things Jesus said that we don't like to hear'.

One of the topics was: 'Sexuality – as it was in the beginning'. I was preaching from Matthew 19 where Jesus speaks about divorce, and I quoted a powerful line Jesus said, that 'it was not [that] way in the beginning' (Matthew 19:8). What amazed me was that after the service, I encountered two responses to my message that I will never forget.

Having taught that, there is only one sexual relationship in the Bible affirmed by God – that between one man and one woman under the binding covenant of biblical marriage – I was utterly humbled when the first person who walked onto the stage, and hugged me for tackling such a tricky topic, turned out to be a bisexual man.

It didn't stop there though; what happened next humbled me even more.

Another man came up to me and told me that he was an elder in a local church and had just come out as a homosexual. Having decided to get away from his own church for a week, he had driven to our area looking for a church where he wouldn't have to think about his situation or even be in a congregation where people knew he was homosexual.

He told me how the first church he went to turned out to be closed for that Sunday. So, he decided to go to a church a couple of miles away in the other direction... oddly, this one was closed too. Reluctantly, as a last resort option he chose to attend our church service.

Now, think that through for one minute.

How many churches in the United Kingdom and possibly the whole world, were choosing to speak that Sunday on the *one subject* that was relevant to him, that he was trying so hard to avoid that morning? What are the odds of the other churches being closed for that *one Sunday*, leading him to come and hear a message on sexuality?

God works in mysterious ways!

The man seemed to appreciate the message even though it did not affirm him in his decision to practise a homosexual relationship. What it did do was to tell him that a church exists, in a neighbourhood not far from his own, with a pastor who doesn't affirm same-sex relationships, yet will seek to love him, welcome him and pastor him, regardless of his sexuality.

A third of the message that day was about love, and how having sound biblical doctrine counts for nothing if you fail to show love to those you are sharing that doctrine with - because Jesus clearly taught us that everything hinges on love. Paul tells us, without love, we are nothing (1 Corinthians 13:2)!

A NOTE OF ENCOURAGEMENT...

Let us start out therefore, with the right foundation in all our discussions on this topic and in all our relationships with the LGBTQ+ community – *let the foundation of all we do be love!*

After all, if Jesus continuously had dinner with and even defended those whose lifestyle He didn't agree with, should not we do likewise?

Jesus' attitude of unprejudiced love led to incredible things: in the case of the woman at the well (John 4) and Zacchaeus (Luke 19), transformation and salvation took place. And, even when confronted with a woman caught in adultery (John 8), Jesus responded by preventing her from being stoned, refusing to condemn her, and instructing her to go away and sin no more!

May we, also, witness and demonstrate such incredible love in all our relationships with the LGBTQ+ community!

Validating the Bible; defining sin

SETTING OUT TERMS

Before we dive into exploring what the Bible says about the same-sex debate, I would like to set out two key things to clarify my own position and challenge you to consider yours.

Firstly, I want to outline why I believe the Bible is infallible as the source and authority from which we can examine the topical issues of sexuality and gender.

Secondly, I want to clarify a definition for what sin actually is.

That way, we can have a strong foundation for discussing what the Bible says.

1. VALIDATING THE BIBLE AS A TRUSTWORTHY SOURCE

Since marrying Rachel, I have had the privilege of driving brand-new cars under her company car scheme.

My previous history of car ownership does nothing to inspire confidence. Over the years, I have owned more than twenty cars, thanks to my method of 'buying them cheap' to avoid borrowing large amounts of money. As you can imagine, you get what you pay for! So, not surprisingly, most ended up dying and being towed away, leaving me with debt accrued through multiple repairs and purchases. When Rachel first wanted to introduce me to her parents, she asked me not to mention my car-swapping habit – I think she thought they would question whether I would take the same approach with my girlfriends! It was sound advice; we are now entering our tenth year of marriage, by the grace of God.

One of the company cars we had the privilege of driving for several years, was a Citroen C4 Grand Picasso. The only annoying thing about this car was the enormous digital speedometer displayed in the centre of the dashboard rather than being in the eye line of the driver only. This meant that every single time I went even one mile per hour over the speed limit, I would get an abrupt warning from my children in the back of the car: "Daddy! You are breaking the law! It's a thirty mile per hour limit here!" It felt as if I had my own built-in police officer condemning me. My first thought was, *Well, it's only* **one** *mile over... come on!*

Yet, the truth is I was still over the limit, and still breaking the law.

There could be no grey area.

Either I was driving legally or illegally.

Now, let's apply this same approach to how we read and view God's Word.

In recent years, when reading about traditional marriage versus the marriage being promoted by modern secular society, there is a growing voice evident in the Church that says, "you can't take Scripture literally". Some theologians have even gone so far as to say that Scripture has been tampered with, therefore we can't rely on it fully or take it literally.

Now, here's the key point: Either we see the Bible as 2 Timothy 3:16-17 endorses it or, we don't. (It really is that simple; there can be no grey to our decision as individuals on this.)

> *All Scripture is God-breathed and is useful for teaching, rebuking, correcting and training in righteousness, so that the servant of God may be thoroughly equipped for every good work.*
>
> (2 Timothy 3:16-17, NIV)

If we hold to the Bible as Paul encourages Timothy to, then we must view it as the holy Word of God; to be revered, feared, and taken seriously in every part of our living. We understand it to be God's Word 'breathed' into being, meaning, whilst it is written by the hands of men, it is inspired by God.

In other words, we need to believe that it is, in fact, *written by God working through men.*

Seen in this light, I would suggest that we handle God's Word carefully and faithfully.

In the same way that there is no grey area between right and wrong when driving to the speed limit, we must ask ourselves: *Can there be a grey area when it comes to the reliability of Scripture?*

Or, put in other words...

If we cannot rely on one part of Scripture, are we not then to call into question all of it? Surely, if it is deemed wrong in one area, it calls into question the whole thing.

A recent article in *Premier Christianity Magazine* called 'Deconstructing Theology' highlights the danger of questioning the integrity of Scripture.[3] The article shines a light on a new trend which encourages the questioning of key biblical doctrines. It claims that by questioning key doctrines in the Bible you can build a better and more palatable faith.[4]

But is this really true?

Whilst questioning our faith is healthy, I suggest that it can be dangerous when we begin to question it in light of our own preferences or base our acceptance of key doctrines on feelings – which is often the case in the sexuality debate.[5] It can be the beginning of a slippery slope towards atheism or deviant Christianity; something that Bart Campolo highlights in the same article:

> *It starts with sovereignty going, then biblical authority goes, then I'm a Universalist, now I'm marrying gay people. Pretty soon I don't believe Jesus actually rose from the dead in a bodily way.[6]*

Whilst the authority and reliability of the Bible is not the primary focus of this book, I do want to give the reader confidence in the reliability of Scripture and the authority of God inherent in it. This is because all that I have written is anchored in the Bible and it is the Bible which constitutes my sole authority and basis for choosing not to affirm same-sex relationships.

Therefore, let me offer a brief and not exhaustive overview of why I believe we can accept and trust the Bible as God's authoritative, reliable and 100% trustworthy instruction for all mankind.

Consistency in number

I have heard it said many times that the Bible has been changed, tampered with, and contains many contradictions.

It is often pointed out that we do not have the original texts - usually, because they were written on short-lasting materials such as animal skin. As copies of the original, it is argued therefore that the surviving manuscripts cannot be trusted with their resulting contradictions and mistakes.

However, let us turn this on its head.

What if I were to say that we have thousands of manuscripts for the Bible and, whilst there are many errors, almost all of them can be whittled down to punctuation and grammatical mistakes rather than contradictions.

In fact, whilst there are thousands of manuscripts with several grammatical typo errors, none of them alter the actual meaning of the text; they all come up with the same doctrinal story and the same message in stating there is only one way to the Father and that it is through Jesus Christ, His one and only begotten Son.

Furthermore, it cannot be denied that the Bible has more manuscripts than exist for any other ancient sources, making it the most attested of ancient writings, with Homer's famed *Iliad* being one of the closest with only approximately 600 surviving copies.

Taken collectively, I would suggest that this leads us to conclude that, rather than being evidence against the reliability of the Bible, the thousands of copies coming up with the same doctrine and story, and pointing to the same truth, stand as evidence *for* the reliability of the Bible.

Proximity to the events

Dating is also strong evidence for the reliability of the Bible.

The Gospels we have today were written just forty to sixty years after the resurrection of Jesus Christ.[7]

Many of the Epistles were recorded even earlier than the Gospels. Some, such as Galatians and Ephesians, were written only fifteen to twenty years after the resurrection, making them highly valuable as sources contemporary to the events they describe – and stronger in this regard than other ancient documents, such as Homer's *Iliad*, whose historical validity has rarely been in question.[8]

The important thing about the records being written so closely in time to the events described within them is that there would have been eyewitnesses still alive who could have disputed the stories if they were fabricated. As such, it is likely that this too would have been recorded as evidence against the historical reliability of the Bible.[9]

The absence of such disputes, therefore, is noticeable!

Archaeological evidence

Another reason we can trust in the validity of the Bible is because it continues to prove its critics wrong in the archaeological world.

The Bible is not a book of tales; it is a history book. It features real people, real locations and real events that are continually verified by historical evidence uncovered by archaeologists.[10] Millar Burrows, Professor of Archaeology at Yale University wrote:

> *On the whole ... archaeological work has unquestionably strengthened confidence in the reliability of the Scriptural*

> record. More than one archaeologist has found his respect for the Bible increased by the experience of excavation in Palestine. Archaeology has in many cases refuted the views of modern critics.[11]

In fact, there is so much archaeological evidence supporting the validity of the Bible (in my opinion, a truly magnificent book) that it should excite anyone who has read it!

And surely, if the archaeological evidence supports the reliability of the places, names and events, we can get even more excited about the reliability of the promises made about Jesus and His free gift of eternal life!

Whilst there is not enough room in this book to share all the archaeological finds, I would like to share some of my favourites...

Sixteen times in the New Testament, a place called Capernaum is mentioned, which is situated by the Sea of Galilee. Over the years since the events of Jesus' time, a fishing village fitting the description of Capernaum in the Gospels has been uncovered. One of the famous stories of the Bible is in Mark 2, where a group of friends carry their lame friend to Jesus for healing. Unable to get through the crowd to Jesus, they climb up onto a roof, break through it and lower their friend down on his mat. In what appears to be Capernaum, houses with flat roofs made of wooden beams and branches have been excavated today, giving a clear example of how these four men could have persevered in bringing their lame friend to Jesus.

Another of my favourite Bible stories is that of the healing at the 'pool near the sheepgate' in John 5. For years, scholars had doubted the reliability of John's Gospel on the basis that this pool did not appear to exist. That is, until the 1930s, when the pool was discovered and excavated with its four colonnades and one across the middle, making five.[12]

In addition to the ongoing uncovering of historical places which feature in the Old and New Testament, there are also many key biblical figures confirmed as historical, real-life individuals through archaeology.

One of these figures is Tiberius Caesar, mentioned in Luke 3. In AD 14-37, the Denarius coin was uncovered showing a portrait of Tiberius Caesar, which perfectly correlates with the chronology of Jesus saying, 'Give back to Caesar what is Caesar's and to God what is God's' (Mark 12:17, NIV).[13]

Then, there's Pontius Pilate who has gone down in history as the man who washed his hands of sentencing Jesus to death by crucifixion. In 1961, an inscription was found where he had lived in Caesarea Maritima, confirming not only that he lived there but also his preferred title used in the Bible of 'Prefect'.[14]

As for the Old Testament... Again, ongoing archaeological discoveries serve to confirm the Bible as historically accurate and reliable.

One of my favourites is the Nabonidus Cylinder.

For many years, there was substantial doubt amongst scholars concerning the book of Daniel, as the name Belshazzar mentioned within it could not be confirmed by any other record. This changed however, when the Nabonidus Cylinder was dug up in 1854 with this inscription found upon it:

> *As for me, Nabonidus, king of Babylon, save me from sinning against your great godhead and grant me as a present a life long of days, and as for **Belshazzar**, the eldest son – my offspring – in still reverence for your great*

godhead in his heart and may he not commit any cultic mistake, may he be sated with a life of plenitude[15]

(My emphasis added)

Now, I could go on, as there are many other examples, however, that is not the purpose of this book.

I only wish to elevate the importance of Scripture and its reliability; not because I say so, but because archaeological evidence *proves* it.

Dead Sea Scrolls as living proof

One of the most exciting discoveries of our time is that of the Dead Sea Scrolls.

In 1947, in Qumran, a village twenty miles east of Jerusalem, a young Bedouin shepherd boy strayed into the mountains to look for his wandering sheep. While there, he decided to throw a stone into one of the caves, resulting in a cracking sound. It was later revealed that his sound was the smashing of a ceramic pot containing leather papyrus scrolls, which would result in the discovery of thousands of fragments of Scripture dating back to the 3rd century BC.[16]

These scrolls contained various Hebrew, Aramaic, and Greek manuscripts, which all confirmed the reliability of the manuscripts that had been used to produce the Bible. In fact, fragments of every Hebrew book of the Old Testament Bible were present within them, save for the book of Esther![17] The Dead Sea Scrolls are dated as being a remarkable one thousand years earlier than any other Old Testament manuscript previously available to us.[18]

What is even more remarkable is that these scroll fragments, preserved for over two thousand years, contain minimal differences from those we already possess, and are consistent with the Bible we know and love today.

This should give us great confidence in the skill and integrity of the scribes down the years who deliberately preserved the words of God's original Scriptures – and even more confidence in our God who has ensured His Word has been passed down through the ages with accuracy. Another key proof that the Bible is the reliable, and trustworthy Word of the one true living God.[19]

Prophetic phenomenon

Hugely exciting though the above all is, for me, the greatest evidence for the reliability of the Bible lies in the sheer audacity of God's prophetic foresight given to us in God's living Word.

The Bible has literally thousands of prophecies contained within it, most of which have been fulfilled to the tee, and only a few hundred that remain yet to be fulfilled in the last days. No other document in history can demonstrate such a miraculous phenomenon!

A personal favourite of mine is the prophecy of King Nebuchadnezzar's dream recorded within the Old Testament book of Daniel (see Daniel 2:31-46).

Nebuchadnezzar has a vivid dream of a large statue made of gold, silver, bronze, iron and clay, which Daniel interprets as four specific future kingdoms – all which would arise and conquer one another before eventually being smashed to pieces by a stone representing Jesus.

What I love about this prophecy is that it not only speaks of the kingdoms that will come after Nebuchadnezzar's reign, it also specifically speaks of a kingdom that will divide into two parts -which is exactly what happened.

This is how most interpret this prophecy as having been fulfilled by the passage of history: The golden head represents the Babylonian kingdom which was conquered by the Medo-Persians (represented in the dream as the chest and arms of silver).[20] Subsequently, the Medo-Persian Empire was taken over by the Greeks when it was defeated in battle by Alexander the Great (represented in the dream as belly and thighs of bronze). Finally, the Roman Empire (represented in the dream as iron legs with feet, partly of iron and partly of baked clay) took over and conquered most of the world. However, the Roman Empire became a divided kingdom in AD 395 – just as is prophesied in verse 41. History attests that the Western Roman Empire fell to the Barbarians within seventy years, whilst the Eastern Roman Empire endured for over a thousand years.[21]

That only leaves the rock – a kingdom established by God Himself, which would destroy all kingdoms in the future. It is this kingdom which excites me most because, according to the prophecy, this kingdom would not be a kingdom of violence, but rather, a kingdom of love. It is this kingdom in Nebuchadnezzar's dream which I believe points people to the everlasting kingdom yet to come, when their King Jesus returns to destroy all other kingdoms and heal the world. This kingdom would be ushered in at Pentecost (Acts 2) and would last for eternity. This kingdom would spread across the whole world conquering hearts until the return of Jesus Christ.

Whilst the Daniel prophecy is only one prophecy, it is worth reiterating that there are thousands more in the Bible, all fulfilled to the tee by history (especially noteworthy are those relating to the virgin birth and Isaiah 53, which points to the suffering Messiah for the forgiveness of sins).

These many prophecies therefore underline not only the historical reliability of the Bible, but also the powerful prophetic witness of Scripture, a phenomenon which cannot be found anywhere else. What other ancient writing in the universe contains prophecies that accurately confirm the passage of history?

Therefore, we can be fully assured that the Bible is reliable and trustworthy, which in turn means we should not take it lightly and we should take its instruction on relationships and marriage very seriously.

Even more importantly, we should get truly excited about the promise of eternity in the presence of a King who loves us and demonstrated this by dying for us on the cross, making it possible for us to have relationship as friends with God Himself.

2. EXPLORING A DEFINITION FOR SIN

A central question we are trying to answer in this book, is whether sexual relationships outside of a marriage between one man and one woman *does constitute sin* in the eyes of God.

This is an important question, because, if the answer is yes, it will need to be acknowledged as a sin and repented of so that individuals may enter into the awesome invitation of relationship with God.

The Bible states that salvation can be found in Christ alone:

> *For the wages of sin is death, but the gift of God*
> *is eternal life in Christ Jesus our Lord.*

(Romans 6:23, NIV)

So, what then is sin?

Put simply, sin is anything that goes against the instruction of God set out in the Holy Scriptures.

We could use one word to sum it up: disobedience.

Or, as Oswald Chambers put it:

> *Sin is not wrongdoing; it is wrong being, deliberate and emphatic independence of God.*[22]

Anything contrary to God's instruction for living is sin, and to attempt to rewrite God's Word to fit our preferences is also a sin. You see, the Word of God serves to liberate us from the world; God never intended that the world should liberate us from God's Word.

One thing I have been pondering is what implications might there be if we were to say that sexual relationships outside of a marriage between one man and one woman were *not* deemed a sin.

For instance, if we opt to overlook certain scriptures on this issue, where do we draw the line? How many other acts of sin are there recorded in the Bible which we could deny in order to live as we choose?

Ultimately, it is vital that we ask, *"What is pleasing to God?"* rather than, *"What is preferable for man?"* Otherwise, surely we have become in authority over Scripture, and are in grave danger of creating a God that we want, rather than honouring the God who actually is...

I cannot count how many times I have met professing Christians who claim they have had revelations that allow them to commit sin.

For instance, I recently had a conversation with a man who told me he believed that God had said it was OK for him to take illegal drugs, and that the Bible does not speak against this notion. Wishing to honour God but also to encourage the man, I was unambiguous in my response: "I'm afraid I do not believe you have heard from God. He would never tell you to do anything that contradicts His Word... Because you see, breaking the law, in this case, would be exactly that."

It is true that many Christians believe there are 'sins' and 'respectable sins', the type that are not that bad. "Surely", they argue, "God won't mind these types of sin?"

Yet, when you read the Bible, this view gets thrown out: sin is sin – and each one of us in God's eyes is culpable as not one of us has managed to lead a sinless life (Romans 3:23).

That said, I do not share the view of many Christians that all sin is the same and there is no ranking system. After all, what did Jesus say to Pilate concerning Pilate's sin and the sin of the Jews?

> Jesus answered, "You would have no power over me if
> it were not given to you from above. Therefore, the one
> who handed me over to you is guilty of a greater sin."

(John 19:11, NIV)

Of course, it is true that a person driving two miles per hour over the speed limit is probably of less interest to the police than someone who commits murder.

Likewise, in the Old Testament Law, does God not instruct that the punishment be proportionate to the crime?

For instance, the Bible makes a distinction between different types of uncleanliness which require different types of sacrifice to be made (Leviticus 11-15). Scripture also distinguishes between and requires different punishment for 'intentional' and 'unintentional' sin in the Old Testament - some of which deserved the death penalty and others that did not (Numbers 15:22-30, Numbers 35:30). Furthermore, there is an unpardonable sin of rejecting the Holy Spirit that is referred to in the Bible, which makes sense because it is the same resurrection power of the Holy Spirit who raised Jesus from the dead who will resurrect us from the dead also. On this count, if we reject the Holy Spirit, resurrection is impossible (Romans 8:11, Ephesians 1:19-20)!

So, whilst it would be an error to say that all sins are of the same depravity, it is important to acknowledge that, in God's eyes, the ultimate punishment for all sin is the same: separation from God (Romans 6:23, Micah 3:4, Isaiah 9:2).

But this is not all.

Crucially, the remedy is also the same: belief in Jesus, followed by repentance, which leads to forgiveness (1 Corinthians 15:17).

Now, let us return to God's Word as the final authority on the matter:

> *For all have sinned and fall short of the glory of God· and all are justified freely by his grace through the redemption that came by Christ Jesus.*

(Romans 3:23, NIV)

For the purposes of this book, then, I will take up the same view of sin that is evident in the Bible:

1. It is God, (not man) who determines what is and what is not sin and has revealed this in His Word.
2. All sin results in separation from God although not all sins are of the same depravity.
3. All sin has the same remedy: Sinners can be redeemed and gloriously forgiven by repenting and believing in Jesus Christ – His death on the cross, His resurrection and His invitation extended to every one of us to receive eternal life.

PART 2

UNCOVERING THE BIBLICAL RECORD

4

A good thing the Law counts for nothing, right?

QUESTIONS THAT NEED ANSWERING

Several years ago, I was asked to teach our youth on what the Bible says about homosexuality and same-sex relationships. This was at a time when the transgender and non-binary movement was not yet in full flow, and the conversation on sexuality was mainly focused on being heterosexual, homosexual or bisexual.

At the end of the meeting, I was approached by one of the girls who regularly attends our youth group – a girl who, for the record, could have her pick of any young man she wanted. Not only is she beautiful on the outside, but she is also equally so on the inside.

She seemed so excited by the session, and she was so thankful to me for saying that our church would never turn away someone on account of their sexuality, even if we do not affirm it. She was overwhelmed almost to tears that I taught the message that we would do as Jesus did in showing love and choosing to journey along with anyone of any sexuality.

As soon as this girl started speaking with such excitement in her voice, I sensed instinctively that she did not consider herself to be heterosexual. It seemed to touch her so deeply. Like a champagne bottle being shaken and released, she was gushing as if the pressure she had been under had finally been released. It didn't take long before I was made aware by several of her friends and family that I was right.

It changes everything when it is someone you have watched grow up and someone you love dearly. It may not have changed my biblical understanding, but this experience increased my compassion greatly towards all those who grapple with this issue.

This set of circumstances also brought new discussions to the table, causing myself and the church leadership to ask key questions we had not asked previously.

Questions like:

Will we allow practicing homosexuals to serve in our church?

And, if they are vocal on social media in a way that goes against our church's core values and statement of belief, how might we address this lovingly?

In the end, still more questions had to be answered:

Is it really a sin these days to be anything other than heterosexual?

Didn't Jesus call us to love all people, regardless?

And is it right not to affirm someone based on their sexuality when they say they were born that way? After all, it's not as if they are harming anyone... How would I like it if someone told me not to fancy my wife?

Effectively, that's what we are doing when we tell a community of people that they must deny what they consider to be their natural impulses towards another consenting human being...

Is this really right and just?

So, to clarify the main questions we are asking here, I want to phrase them in other words:

1. Is anything other than heterosexual relationships a sin according to the Bible?
2. Is the Law of God still relevant when it comes to the LGBTQ+ debate in the Church?

I hear you say, "I mean, of course the Law of God is clear on this, but we are no longer under the Law but under grace, right? So, the Law doesn't count anymore on this sexuality issue, surely?"

We'll consider these two questions in this chapter because it is vital that we get to the bottom of this.

SURELY, THE LAW IS DONE AWAY WITH?

Some key verses in Leviticus say:

If a man has sexual relations with a man as one does with a woman, both of them have done what is detestable. They are to be put to death; their blood will be on their own heads.

(Leviticus 20:13, NIV)

Do not have sexual relations with a man as one does with a woman; that is detestable.

(Leviticus 18:22, NIV)

37

Anyone reading these verses in Leviticus, at face value, will find it hard to deny that God is not pleased by same-gender sexual relationships.

In fact, these very verses with such inflammatory language could steer many professed homosexuals away from Christianity, and even those heterosexuals who may sympathise with the homosexual community.

But the question remains... Does the Law still apply now that we are under grace as is expressed in Romans 6:14 (NIV) by the apostle Paul:

> *For sin shall no longer be your master, because*
> *you are not under the law, but under grace.*

Paul takes this even further in Galatians 5:1 (NIV), saying:

> *It is for freedom that Christ has set us free,*
> *stand firm, then, and do not let yourselves be*
> *burdened again by a yoke of slavery.*

Furthermore, this raises yet another question:

Should Christians with my view towards homosexuality examine whether they are hypocritical?

I cannot deny that there are other laws listed within the Old Testament Law of God which I do not keep and do not intend to (and I'm sure this applies to other Christians too). For instance, the Law also forbids those observing it to wear clothes made from two different materials (Leviticus 19:19).

How many of us follow this particular law, I wonder?

In his book, *God and the Gay Christian*, Matthew Vines asks a reasonable question on this matter:

*Why do Christians find it easy to disregard most of the law,
yet hold to the law on prohibiting homosexual practice?*[23]

It's a fair point, one which we will unpack in this chapter.

I wonder, would those of us who hold to Leviticus, as our reasoning for not accepting homosexuality, shudder if we were to read James 2:10? A verse where James starkly reminds his readers that, if you hold to one part of the Law, you'd better hold to the lot:

> *For whoever keeps the whole law and yet stumbles
> at just one point is guilty of breaking all of it.*

So, the real question behind this issue is whether the Law *does* still apply to Christians today?

Some of it, all of it, or none of it?

Galatians 3:19 (NIV) says:

> *Why, then, was the law given at all? It was
> added because of transgressions until the Seed
> to whom the promise referred had come.*

So, this verse would imply that the Law was only given until Jesus, the seed of Abraham appeared (see Galatians 3:16). Can we then accept the interpretation that the Law was abolished with Jesus and that the conservative view of homosexuality as something sinful in God's eyes is no longer relevant?

I think it is key to look at Jesus' words regarding the Law as the final authority on the matter:

> *Do not think that I have come to abolish the Law or the
> Prophets; I have not come to abolish them but to fulfil them.*

> (Matthew 5:17, NIV)

Now, many would say that Jesus has completed the Law and done what we could not, and that He conquered it on the cross. However, if God in His wisdom chose these laws to be the code for human life, why would He suddenly do away with them and change them, particularly in regard to Leviticus 20:13 and Leviticus 18:22?

Are we to claim that what was an abomination to God thousands of years ago has suddenly changed?

Has God changed His mind?

Did the LORD lie to the prophet Malachi when He said to him:

> *I the LORD do not change? So, you, the descendants of Jacob, are not destroyed.*

(Malachi 3:6, NIV)

It would seem to me that Scripture does not lie, and God does not change. It would also seem to me that logically, if God does not change and He was not for homosexuality yesterday, then logically, He is not for it today.

So, let's return to the Law with this understanding of God's unchangeable nature.

Is it still relevant to us?

Some of it?

All of it?

None of it?

GOD'S HOLINESS CODE

It's worth noting that the part of the Law which deals with homosexuality is known as the part that deals with the Holiness

Code – which arose in Old Testament times concerning ritual purity.

Some have tried to suggest that the Holiness Code began in response to idolatry, which included child prostitution practised in the surrounding nations.[24] However, the problem with this idea is that firstly, it cannot be proven true, and secondly, it cannot eradicate the consistent message in Scripture that does not affirm same-sex relationships. The Holiness Code of which Leviticus 20:13 and 18:13 are a part, actually flows out of Leviticus 19:2.[25]

Speak to the entire assembly of Israel and say to them:
"Be holy because I, the LORD your God, am holy."

(Leviticus 19:2, NIV)

God gave these laws which form the Holiness Code to ensure that His people, Israel, kept themselves pure from the unholy practices of the surrounding nations. They were to stand out as different and holy, something that we see echoed by Jesus when He instructed His followers to be the light of the world, a city on a hill that cannot be hidden (Matthew 5:14).

John Richardson points out in his book, *What God Has Made Clean*, that the Law was always intended to be temporary, until the coming of the Messiah (whom the Law pointed to), and that much of the Law would be completed once and for all in Him, Jesus Christ.[26] He states that the Law was made up of three different elements that played a different role, referring to ceremonial laws, civil laws and moral laws.[27]

First, Richardson points out that there were ceremonial laws for the atonement of sin which were conducted by the priests on behalf of the people. However, these ceremonial laws came to their completion in Christ as is confirmed by Hebrews 10:8-10 (NIV):

> First he said, "Sacrifices and offerings, burnt offerings
> and sin offerings you did not desire, nor were you pleased
> with them"– though they were offered in accordance
> with the law. Then he said, "Here I am, I have come to do
> your will." He sets aside the first to establish the second.
> And by that will, we have been made holy through the
> sacrifice of the body of Jesus Christ once for all.

Next, there were the civil laws, which included commands such as clothes must not contain two kinds of material woven together or laws on how to deal with incidents where negligence had led to death, and many others too numerous to cite in their entirety here. Richardson concludes that these laws were only for the immediate benefit of the nation of Israel; that they might be set apart from other nations as evidenced in Exodus 19:5 (NIV):

> Now if you obey me fully and keep my covenant,
> then out of all nations you will be my treasured
> possession. Although the whole earth is mine.

So, ceremonial laws were accomplished by Jesus in His sacrifice, being the once-and-for-all atonement, the sacrificial Lamb of God who takes away the sin of the world, affirmed by John 1:29 (NIV):

> The next day John saw Jesus coming toward him and said,
> "Look, the Lamb of God, who takes away the sin of the world!"

This means we no longer require the regular religious rituals performed on our behalf by a priest – which would have occurred in the Old Testament times. They have been made redundant as Jesus, the great High Priest, has become for us the once-and-for-all sacrificial lamb; making us holy by the shedding of His precious blood and inviting us into the

'Most Holy Place', which we enter into by faith and repentance (Hebrews 10:19, NIV).

The third sets of laws, in contrast to the other two, were the moral laws, and Leviticus 20:13 is included as one of them. Alongside outlining the Holiness Code, these moral laws also dealt with a sense of fair practice when trading with others (Leviticus 19:36). Such laws were not only instructions, but importantly, they revealed part of God's character which He intended His people to imitate and to continue to abide by.

As Richardson states, the way in which believers today are to follow these moral laws is not to be as a Pharisee, prescribing a legalistic tick-the-box way of life. Rather, it is by living out a life which celebrates, honours and demonstrates God's kingdom-character through genuine commitment to Christ Jesus.

It was Christ, who brought an end to the written Law, and in doing so would bring about a new obedience of the heart, explained by Paul (who himself originally came from a Pharisee background) in Romans 2:15 (NIV):[28]

> *They show that the requirements of the law are written on their hearts, their consciences also bearing witness, and their thoughts sometimes accusing them and at other times even defending them.*

This wasn't a new thing dreamt up by Paul either; the prophets spoke of it hundreds of years in advance of Jesus' birth and ministry:

Ezekiel recognised it.

I will give you a new heart and put a new spirit in you; I will remove from you your heart of stone and give you a heart of flesh.

(Ezekiel 36:26, NIV)

So did Jeremiah.

"This is the covenant I will make with the people of Israel after that time" declares the LORD. "I will put my law in their minds and write it on their hearts. I will be their God, and they will be my people."

(Jeremiah 31:33, NIV)

And the same message occurs in Hebrews, in the New Testament:

This is the covenant I will make with them after that time, says the Lord. I will put my laws in their hearts, and I will write them on their minds.

(Hebrews 10:16, NIV)

Is the Law done away with today?

The Ceremonial Law? Yes!

The Civil Law? For sure!

But what about the Moral Laws which reveal the character of God? No way!

We have seen that God's recurring message in the Bible is that these Moral Laws have been written on the heart of every believer, and it is by living by the Law of the Spirit that we can be closer to God and filled with His Holy Spirit. It is by living a life where we do not grieve the Holy Spirit. It is why Jesus addresses the heart of the believer in the Sermon on the Mount (Matthew 6-8). God still expects every believer to live by His moral Holiness Code; when a believer does this, they are, as Paul says in Romans, 'a law for themselves':

(Indeed, when Gentiles, who do not have the law, do by nature things required by the law, they are a law for themselves, even though they do not have the law. They show that the requirements of the law are written on their hearts, their consciences also bearing witness, and their thoughts sometimes accusing them and at other times even defending them.) This will take place on the day when God judges people's secrets through Jesus Christ, as my gospel declares.

(Romans 2:14-16, NIV)

What Paul is saying is that when a believer who is not under the written Law, lives a life which flows from the Holiness Code *within* the Law, they are honouring God. Not because they are told to in obeying a specific written law, but because they are *choosing* to do so out of relationship with the Holy Spirit. 'Their consciences also bearing witness, and their thoughts sometimes accusing them' (Romans 2:15, NIV) – this is the witness and guidance of the Holy Spirit in the life of a believer.

It is what is known as being Spirit-led or 'life in the Spirit' which is something Paul repeatedly talks of throughout his letters to the Church (see Galatians 5:16-18, NIV).

Based on what we have considered regarding the Law, I believe it would be dangerous to say that Leviticus 20:13 can be ignored: As this would constitute rejecting a moral law which reveals part of God's character and design for His creation, something we will explore further in subsequent chapters.

A NOTE OF CHALLENGE...

All this brings me to say, it has become far too easy to paint conservative believers with a brush of either being so-called legalistic and prejudiced in their attitudes, or utterly lacking in love and compassion.

Is this really true – or a fair judgment of such individuals?

Do pastors and individuals keeping to this conservative view set out to be prejudiced, to be legalistic and unloving?

I doubt it.

As I have already stated in this book, personally, I would love to be able to affirm same-sex relationships. It would be so easy to do it and would mean I was never in a place where I could be accused of a lack of compassion when it came to a question of sexuality.

However, when I read the Bible, I cannot find permission to do so anywhere. In fact, there doesn't seem to be anything positive said about same-sex relationships at all.

For this reason, I am left with the same decision that Peter and the apostles made in Acts 5:29 (NIV):

> Peter and the other apostles replied: "We must
> obey God rather than human beings!"

Proverbs 9:10 (NIV) says, 'The fear of God is the beginning of wisdom', yet I wonder if this is something we are really living out in today's international church doctrine?

It saddens me hugely to say exactly the opposite; that so many churches and believers seem to have *lost* their fear of God. They appear to be willing to throw aside the Word of God and to compromise on what it says in order to make friends with culture.

Is this the correct approach?

Surely, God should come *before* culture?

I believe that God is calling us to ensure we keep Him in His rightful position, as God and Lord of our lives.

Let's not sidestep the fact that:

He is God Almighty, *not 'God all-matey'*!

Therefore, before we run ahead with the vision to fill our churches no matter the compromises to our walk with Jesus, let us first ask ourselves how we can ensure our churches continue to be filled with His Holy Spirit; that we neither quench His Spirit nor deny His instruction.

The Christian life was never meant to be easy.

One of the most controversial things Jesus told His followers is that the world would hate them (and us), His Church, just as it hated Him:

> *If the world hates you, keep in mind that it hated me first. If you belonged to the world, it would love you as its own. As it is, you do not belong to the world, but I have chosen you out of the world. That is why the world hates you.*
>
> (John 15:18-19, NIV)

Therefore, we must be two things simultaneously: wise in what we do embrace *yet* loving and compassionate in what we do not.

The Law does not count for nothing in our New Testament covenant lives.

It still counts for everything because the part of the Law which outlines God's Holiness Code is as important today as it was in Old Testament times.

The question is whether we are willing to take it seriously and allow God to take our sometimes-hardened hearts and shape them after Himself?

5

Jesus had nothing to say on the issue, right?

PREACHING THE WHOLE TRUTH

One of the most common arguments on alternative relationships to that of one man and one woman is the view that Jesus never actually spoke against it, therefore He must be OK with it.

"After all, doesn't loving our neighbour mean accepting whatever they choose to do with their lives? In this vein, anyone opposing same-sex relationships is effectively a modern-day Pharisee, trying to impose irrelevant legalism and law on another individual. Plus, let's not forget that Jesus spent most of His time *opposing* such legalistic people."

I'm sure that either you have heard this argument before or used it yourself...

Well, let me be completely honest with you: I have spent so much time agonising and praying on exactly this scenario, and I have zero desire to be deemed a Pharisee! I have told God that I really **don't** want to do what Jesus warned us not to do:

> *If anyone causes one of these little ones—those*
> *who believe in me   to stumble, it would be better*
> *for them if a large millstone were hung around*
> *their neck, and they were thrown into the sea.*

> (Mark 9:42, NIV)

I don't want to cause anyone to stumble in their walk with Christ regardless of age, ethnicity or gender etc.

I've prayed on this topic and asked God a terrifying question: *What if my view of sexuality is turning people away from Jesus?*

It's a possibility that literally petrifies me!

Then, at the same time, I think to myself, something like this...

But, God, if I teach the wrong gospel and misinterpret the Bible (perhaps because I want to make it easier for people to enter heaven) then surely, I'm in an even greater danger?

One of the things that helps me in this situation is to remind myself that the gospel is not about getting people into heaven; it's about getting heaven into people. Or, put another way: The gospel is not about getting people into the kingdom of God, it's about getting the kingdom of God into people.

So, how do we do this? It's actually very simple and means highlighting four key things to individuals:

1. All people have turned to their own ways rather than living as God originally intended for us: this is what the Bible calls sin.
2. However, His one and only Son, Jesus, became a man, walked the earth, died on a cross to pay the penalty for our sin, and rose to life three days later conquering death.

3. That if anyone believes what I have just written, turns back to God and sincerely asks for forgiveness, He will forgive their sins and grant them eternal life.
4. God will then send His Holy Spirit to live within them, to guide, equip and empower them to live a new life honouring to Him.

This transformation is expressed further in Romans 12:2 (NIV) which says:

Do not conform to the pattern of this world but be transformed by the renewing of your mind. Then you will be able to test and approve what God's will is—his good, pleasing and perfect will. Interestingly, I hear this verse thrown around a lot in church as though it were a proof text confirming the instant transformation that takes place when becoming a Christian. In reality, it's a verse intended for all of us as believers in our ongoing journeys becoming more like Jesus; to invite the Holy Spirit daily to help us in aligning ourselves with God's will rather than the will of the world. It requires cooperation with the Holy Spirit, and it involves sacrificing our old way of life for a new way of life in the Spirit:

For the law of the Spirit of life in Christ Jesus has made me free.

(Romans 8:2, NKJV)

It's not about shaping the kingdom of God in such a way that men and women can receive it; it's about a supernatural reshaping of the human heart so that they are willing to embrace the kingdom *at any cost.*

We can see this in Jesus' teaching when He shared the parable of the Precious Pearl and the willingness of the man featured in it to sell everything he had. Only then was he able to take hold of the precious pearl which represented the overwhelmingly precious kingdom of God (Matthew 13:45-56).

Are you willing to give up anything for this eternal kingdom or, more importantly, for your relationship with God now and into the future?

It may cost you all your money, your ambitions, your comfort zones, perhaps even be detrimental to your health as it was for Paul and Peter... It may even cost you your sexuality.

That's something to stop and consider, isn't it?

And I don't discount myself from that scenario. What if God had asked me to remain celibate and make a deliberate choice *not* to fancy my wife when I was considering searching for a life partner? Would I have had the guts to accept that eventuality? And just because He did not, does that mean it is fair of me to expect others to do something that seemingly goes against their inclinations for their own future happiness?

I can't ask that of you, myself; but I can point you to Jesus. I wonder what He is asking you to give up for Him.

SO, JESUS NEVER SPOKE ABOUT SAME-SEX RELATIONSHIPS... DOES THAT MEAN HE'S OK WITH THEM?

Well, Jesus never spoke about taking drugs... so, is it OK? He spoke about giving back to Caesar what was Caesar's, yet He never directly condemned offshore tax evasion (see Mark 12:17). He never spoke about incest... so, is that OK? Well, while most would probably say, "No, absolutely not!", let me throw something controversial into the mix. In the age we live in where we often hear 'love is love', if it's a case of two consenting adults... in theory, incest should be OK, right?

OK, so you see where I am going with this.

Jesus didn't *directly* speak about many things. Yet, this doesn't mean He approves of them in our lives today.

A friend of mine who has a Doctorate in Theology was asked the question recently, "What are we meant to continue to obey from the Old Testament if we are under a new covenant of grace?" My friend's answer was profound. He said, "Well, if it's in the Old Testament and we are meant to continue with it, you'll find it in the New Testament."

My first thought was *Hmm, that sounds a bit too simplistic, and I don't think it'll work.* However, I was proven wrong when I started looking for myself. Let me assure you, it's a very reliable litmus test. I recommend you try reading the Bible with my friend's approach in mind, it's truly eye-opening!

That's pretty much where we get to with Jesus on the same-sex relationships question. He doesn't stand on a mountain and directly say, "Thou shalt not lie with someone of the same sex." However, He does get drawn into a conversation on marriage and divorce, and His response is very helpful indirectly on this topic of same-sex relationships.

Jesus on marriage and divorce

Let's look at what Jesus says in Matthew 19:1-12 (NIV):

When Jesus had finished saying these things, he left Galilee and went into the region of Judea to the other side of the Jordan. Large crowds followed him, and he healed them there. Some Pharisees came to him to test him. They asked, "Is it lawful for a man to divorce his wife for any and every reason?"

"Haven't you read," he replied, "that at the beginning the Creator 'made them male and female,' and said, 'For this reason a man will leave his father and mother and be united to his wife, and the two will become one flesh'? So, they are no longer two, but one flesh. Therefore, what God has joined together, let no one separate." "Why then," they asked, "did Moses command that a man give his wife a certificate of divorce and send her away?"

Jesus replied, "Moses permitted you to divorce your wives because your hearts were hard. But it was not this way from the beginning. I tell you that anyone who divorces his wife, except for sexual immorality, and marries another woman commits adultery."

The disciples said to him, "If this is the situation between a husband and wife, it is better not to marry."

Jesus replied, "Not everyone can accept this word, but only those to whom it has been given. For there are eunuchs who were born that way, and there are eunuchs who have been made eunuchs by others—and there are those who choose to live like eunuchs for the sake of the kingdom of heaven. The one who can accept this should accept it."

It's helpful to start by considering the context of this passage.

The Pharisees were looking to trap Jesus in a debate of their day as there were two schools of thought that were circulating at the time. Whilst some followed the teaching of Rabbi Shammia, who held a stricter, more traditional view of marriage which permitted divorce only for marital unfaithfulness, others followed the teaching of Rabbi Hillel. In contrast to Shammia, Hillel took a more relaxed view whereby divorce could be obtained for reasons of minor disappointment with the wife's performance in her duties. Hillel's line of thought was to say that something as simple as not performing well in her domestic tasks, provided just cause for a husband to request a divorce.

By questioning Jesus on this subject, therefore, the Pharisees deliberately sought to expose and trap him into saying something that would not please his listeners. The Pharisees knew that, had He sided with Rabbi Shammia and his strict views on divorce, Jesus would have been unpopular with the many men at that time who wanted to be able to divorce for any reason they chose. On the other hand, they knew also that if He opted to side with Rabbi Hillel, He could be accused of having a relaxed view of Scriptures that had been handed down to the Jews by Moses. Either way, it seemed they could trap Him easily – or so they thought.

That's a bit of the context but what is more important with regards to our question of Jesus' take on same-sex attraction, is His response to the Pharisees. It's really valuable that Jesus says several things in this passage relevant to our topic of understanding what relationships are affirmed by God.

In verse 4, Jesus does something very important for us; He begins His explanation by pointing His listeners back to Adam and Eve. He affirms His belief in the Genesis account as being literal and not allegoric. He also affirms that we are 'made male and female'; that this was God's original blueprint before sin entered the world and corrupted His good and pleasing creation.

Then, in verse 6, Jesus gives us an understanding of the way we were created to be. He talks clearly of *one male and one female coming together*, cleaving from the parents, and becoming one flesh; two key, distinct ingredients of masculine and feminine DNA, which, we can all concede are necessary in order to conceive and bear a child. It is the creative order that cannot work in any other way. It means sex is both a physical and spiritual act, and Jesus affirms this relationship saying, 'What God joins, let no man separate' (v.6). So, we can see that faced with the question of relationships and divorce etc, Jesus points back to the beginning. He directly affirms the blueprint of a relationship between one man and one woman, and it is important for us to recognise that it is the *only* sexual relationship between two people affirmed and spoken of positively in the whole of Scripture.

In verse 8, Jesus also says something very important in His reply to why Moses first permitted divorce. He starts by addressing the heart of the people listening, telling them that their hearts are hard. But then He continues and says something easy to overlook but vital: 'but it was not this way from the beginning' (v.8).

Jesus unapologetically tells the religious leaders that their hard hearts have caused them to sin and break God's original blueprint set out in the beginning. Then, He goes on to tell them the bottom line: 'I tell you that anyone who divorces his wife, except for sexual immorality, and marries another woman commits adultery' (v.9).

The first thing we learn from Jesus here, is that, whilst He doesn't directly speak of same-sex relationships, He does challenge wrong teaching on relationships and divorce. Even more importantly, He challenges wrong teaching by pointing to the way it was in the beginning.

In other words, if you want the right answer to what a *biblical marriage* is, look at the model of the male and female who God joined together, blessed, and commanded to multiply on the earth in Genesis.

The only reason the world goes astray from this blueprint is because the human heart is corrupted by sin... *hard hearts.*

Now, it should be explained at this point, if you stand for relationships between one man and one woman, then you also need to be fair across the board. It would be extremely unfair to overlook the question of heterosexual sexual relationships before marriage or living together, for instance. And, in fact, the view of divorce in the Church needs to be reviewed and acted on according to Scripture, something I have been pondering repeatedly in my heart. It's so easy to talk about the debate of the day being same-sex relationships when, in fact, we may find we have a hypocritical view on other areas between heterosexuals, such as those mentioned in this paragraph.

The purpose of my book is to specifically consider same-sex relationships, but it would be remiss of me to omit this, so I wish briefly to say that *all of us in the Church are accountable for our actions before God.*

This means we all have a responsibility to choose His 'good, pleasing and perfect will' (Romans 12:2, NIV) for our lives if we are sincere in our commitment to let Him be Lord of our lives. For those who are not yet married, to choose either to co-habit or engage in sexual relations, therefore, is to act contrary to this.

Now, it doesn't end there, though.

Jesus on eunuchs

In verse 10, the Pharisees find this teaching hard to swallow and confess it would be better not to marry at all than to live with such demands. To which Jesus gives another profound response, which can contribute further to our thinking around same-sex relationships.

After affirming relationships between one man and one woman as ordained by God in the beginning, and then rejecting divorce on the basis of men's whims, Jesus continues by giving an alternative option... Jesus says: 'Not everyone can accept this word, but only those to whom it has been given. For there are eunuchs who were born that way, and there are eunuchs who have been made eunuchs by others—and there are those who choose to live like eunuchs for the sake of the kingdom of heaven. The one who can accept this should accept it' (v.10).

56

Not everyone can accept this word!

Not everyone can handle relationships as set out in the beginning between one man and one woman.

Not everyone can cope with the idea that only in marital unfaithfulness may a divorce be granted.

Yet, Jesus goes on to give the only other option for those who cannot accept His teaching on the Genesis blueprint of one man and one woman.

He uses a eunuch as a figurative term for someone who voluntarily abstains from sexual relationships and marriage for 'the sake of the kingdom of heaven' and presents three different types of eunuch. First, He concedes that that there are some who are born eunuchs meaning they were born without genitalia required for having sexual relations. Then, He talks of others who have been made eunuchs meaning they are forced by others not to have sexual relationships and marry. Finally, He refers to one other eunuch and it is this type which needs to be highlighted here, because it is especially relevant in considering the Church's interaction with today's growing LGBTQ+ community. Jesus speaks of those who choose to live like eunuchs, 'those that choose to stay celibate for the sake of the kingdom of heaven' (v.12).

In other words, Jesus describes individuals who choose a path without marriage and without sex who choose deliberately to pursue the kingdom of God, to follow God's instruction and God's purpose for their lives.

True, Jesus may never have spoken directly of same-sex relationships; however, as scholars like Grenz state, He *did* speak of those who would lay down their personal sexual desires for relationships to pursue a kingdom-life that honours, pleases and serves the Lord.[29]

So, the answer is, Jesus *does* address same-sex relationships indirectly in this passage by affirming what marriage is, and what we should do if that marriage model is not for us.[30]

A NOTE OF ENCOURAGEMENT...

Now, I know this is not an easy thing for all of us to read or accept, so I want to give a word both of warning and encouragement. Anyone who finds it easy to point the finger at those in same sex-relationships should be careful and kind. How would anyone like to have loving desires towards someone and be told they cannot enter that relationship? It's basically like telling a husband they are no longer allowed to be with their wife. It's painful – of that we cannot be in doubt! And those who choose the kingdom over their earthly desires for a relationship should be loved and supported with incredible compassion.

Furthermore, I believe that anyone who chooses to be celibate for the sake of the kingdom of God deserves a heavenly commendation and a greater crown (see James 1:12, Revelation 2:10) than anyone like me who has feelings for the opposite sex and is allowed to marry the wife of my dreams.

Whilst I write this book and believe in what I write, I have wrestled so much with the burdens that this likely brings to many – and can only imagine the pain it must involve.

If you, reader, are among those struggling, I want you to know that you are truly on my heart.

May you know that I am totally for you, as your brother in Christ.

By no means do I want to underestimate the sacrifice you are facing as you grapple with this issue of what Jesus says concerning same-sex attraction.

So may the words of Jesus encourage you – as only He can:

And everyone who has left houses or brothers or sisters or father or mother or wife or children or fields for my sake will receive a hundred times as much and will inherit eternal life.

(Matthew 19:29, NIV)

Paul on same-sex relationships and signs of the times

SIGNS OF THE TIMES?

Food for thought from 2 Timothy 3:1-5...

Remember that lengthy discussion I had with my wife? The one that passed through our Clapham Junction kitchen? (You'll know what I'm talking about if you managed to read the Introduction.) Well, that conversation got me thinking about what the New Testament says when it comes to LGBTQ+ and the times we are living in, especially about what the apostle Paul says...

One passage especially sticks in my mind.

Paul says, in 2 Timothy 3:1-5 (NIV):

> *But mark this: There will be terrible times in the last days. People will be lovers of themselves, lovers of money, boastful, proud, abusive, disobedient to their parents, ungrateful, unholy, without love, unforgiving,*

> *slanderous, without self-control, brutal, not lovers of the*
> *good, treacherous, rash, conceited, lovers of pleasure*
> *rather than lovers of God—having a form of godliness but*
> *denying its power. Have nothing to do with such people.*

You don't need to look too hard to see that this scripture can apply to our day (although, granted, it could apply to many other generations, too). Even so, the characteristics of people listed above all seem to feature in our society today.

Lovers of self? Just look at the advent of social media enabling people to idolise self like never before - with endless selfies and visuals of 'our best self' constantly clogging up our screens (which, let's face it, can often be a mask for our true selves and struggles).

Lovers of money? Well, let's consider the impact of internet giants like Amazon, acting as vehicles to satisfy instant gratification, bringing things to your doorstep 24/7 at the click of a finger. Or look at the popularity of financial credit that is based on figures on a screen, not bank notes stored away.

Disobedience to parents? I don't think anyone would dispute the fact that the average modern-day family often lacks in discipline and many children have limited respect for their parents... In fact, I was reading recently of an 11-year-old child in Orlando, Florida, who took his parents to court to gain a divorce from them so that he could be fostered. Can you imagine that?

I will leave you to look through the list and prayerfully decide if you think it sounds familiar, but for now, let's skip to verse 5: 'having a form of godliness but denying its power.'

We live in a time where many of the worldly campaigns have a so-called 'form of godliness' about them. They promote the welfare of the oppressed, and rightly so. Regardless of belief about acceptable practices, every human being must be loved and respected.

However, sometimes, something unfortunate can happen – even if not originally intended. What may start off with the admirable objective of rallying support and raising awareness of the need for love and respect for certain oppressed groups can quickly turn into something different. What about the eventuality where those very groups in turn become the oppressor and start pushing through their cause in an aggressive manner?

Sadly, it does happen.

Think about it and ask yourself this question: What were the two issues in the news of sport over the summer of 2021 that dominated the media?

Who didn't take the knee; are they racist?

And who didn't wear the rainbow armbands; are they homophobic?

Personally, I would be in favour of taking the knee, but I would not wish to wear the armbands, on the basis that I believe to do so would run contrary to God's Word. Let me explain...

Wearing rainbow armbands may seem a perfectly innocent way to show kindness and love towards another human being – surely, a good thing, right? In fact, some might say showing such support could be seen as a form of "godliness", as it is a form of social justice – standing up for an oppressed minority.

Yet, should I, as a Christian, support a movement that contradicts what I believe the Bible says? Surely, this would deny the power and truth of Scripture.

Could it be, that more than ever before, our modern-day society has become like the one described in 2 Timothy 3?

Now, this isn't to say that a Christian can't show love and respect towards the LGBTQ+ community whilst also holding to a traditional biblical view of marriage.

At the same time, it's important to ask another question:

Will society and the LGBTQ+ movement show the same love and respect towards Christians who respectfully and lovingly uphold these beliefs?

It's certainly worth pausing to consider.

Food for thought from Romans 1:18-32...

Paul says in Romans 1:18-32 (NIV):

The wrath of God is being revealed from heaven against all the godlessness and wickedness of people, who suppress the truth by their wickedness, since what may be known about God is plain to them, because God has made it plain to them. For since the creation of the world God's invisible qualities—his eternal power and divine nature—have been clearly seen, being understood from what has been made, so that people are without excuse.

For although they knew God, they neither glorified him as God nor gave thanks to him, but their thinking became futile, and their foolish hearts were darkened. Although they claimed to be wise, they became fools and exchanged the glory of the immortal God for images made to look like a mortal human being and birds and animals and reptiles.

Therefore, God gave them over in the sinful desires of their hearts to sexual impurity for the degrading of their bodies with one another. They exchanged the truth about God for a lie and worshipped and served created things rather than the Creator—who is forever praised. Amen.

Because of this, God gave them over to shameful lusts. Even their women exchanged natural sexual relations for unnatural ones. In the same way the men also abandoned natural relations with women and were inflamed with lust for one another. Men committed shameful acts with other men and received in themselves the due penalty for their error.

These verses, from Paul's letter to the Church of Rome, are the clearest message I can find in his teaching regarding our question of sexuality and same-sex relationships. However, before we unpack what he says, I want to draw your attention to an important factor that once more gives me reason to pause and ponder whether we are alert to signs of the times. Paul says in verse 24:

Therefore, God gave them over *in the sinful desires of their hearts to sexual impurity for the degrading of their bodies with one another.* (my emphasis added)

As I meditated on this scripture, 'God gave them over,' another passage came to mind: the events in Exodus 9:12, when God hardened Pharoah's heart further and further before he eventually permitted the Israelites to leave Egypt and their oppression as slave-workers. In this scenario, Pharoah was already grieving God by treating His people badly. So, God hardened his heart or, we could say, 'gave him over' to his own sinful desires.

Then, as I pondered further, the verse of Acts 17:19 also came to mind, when Paul was in Athens and addressed the Athenians who were obsessed with idols. I looked it up and these words stood out to me immediately:

*In the past **God overlooked such ignorance**, but **now he commands all people everywhere to repent**.* (my emphasis added)

Much like Romans 1, the issue, here, begins with idols and ends up with the people having an 'unknown God', applicable to us as I'm sure we would agree there are many such 'gods' in our days. In contrast to Romans 1 where we have seen that God 'gave [the people] over,' Acts 17:19 says that God 'overlooked' their sin for a time but, as Paul emphasises, now there is a gear shift as Paul declares God is calling '[everyone] everywhere to repent'.

I've begun to wonder whether these scriptures can be seen as not just relevant to our times today, but actually, accurately describing our twenty-first century world. Has God overlooked the sinful behaviour of our society and effectively 'given the world over' to its sinful desires *in our time?*

I have also begun to wonder whether the chaos in the world from the impact of wars, rumours of wars, strange weathers (climate change rubberstamps the reality of these), famines, and plagues including a worldwide pandemic, has something to do with the increased ungodliness that is at the root of the many things we seem so concerned to champion... things like LGBTQ+ campaigns, abortion or assisted dying - to name a few. Could it be that whilst these campaigns have been growing fast in recent years, God has 'overlooked' them for a time and given us over to our sinful desires?

Could it be also that now, He is calling everyone, everywhere, to repent?

I wonder... is it fair to say that, often, the only way people will stop, and think is when something goes wrong? Such as a war or a pandemic, perhaps?

You might say, "Well, hang on Mike, are you really saying that you believe God would send a pandemic? That just doesn't seem like something God would do!"

Yet, God has done so in the past... Why would He not do so again? I think of Moses and Pharoah and the Plagues. Or what about the words of Jeremiah 24:10 echoed in those of Jeremiah 29:16-19?

> But this is what the LORD says about the king who sits on David's throne and all the people who remain in this city, your fellow citizens who did not go with you into exile—yes, this is what the LORD Almighty says: "I will send the sword, famine and plague against them and I will make them like figs that are so bad they cannot be eaten. I will pursue them with the sword, famine and plague and will make them abhorrent to all the kingdoms of the earth, a curse and an object of horror, of scorn and reproach, among all the nations where I drive them. For they have not listened to my words," declares the LORD, "words that I sent to them again and again by my servants the prophets. (Jeremiah 29:16-19, NIV)

It sounds strange and a bit 'un-Christian' to say that God sends sword, famine, and plagues, doesn't it? But listen to what God says in Jeremiah 18:7-8 (NIV):

> If at any time I announce that a nation or kingdom is to be uprooted, torn down and destroyed, and if that nation I warned repents of its evil, then I will relent and not inflict on it the disaster I had planned.

God does not desire to harm the nations; He desires, as Acts 17:19 puts it, 'for everyone everywhere to repent'. God wants to bless the nations but, as a just God He cannot do that whilst they choose to reject His word and worse, play God with His creation, thereby leading future generations astray.

That said, some questions begin to form in my mind...

Do I believe God is sending pandemics and wars upon the world right now, because the nations have rejected His Word?

Do I believe that all the calamities and disasters already listed earlier in this chapter are God's divine wrath for us, in our time?

Honestly, in my heart, I'm not sure these events are being sent directly by God... Unless we really have reached the time of the Tribulation and the horsemen of the Apocalypse depicted in Revelation. At the very least it doesn't feel right, despite what I have written above. I will touch on this more in the chapter on Chastisement, but for now, let's hold in tension the image of God as Almighty and sovereign over all things and God as all-loving and desirous to be compassionate and merciful, even amid apparent disaster or judgment.

Could it be that in our time, something different is going on? God wants all to repent and so is providing an opportunity for common grace for all?

Now a word of warning and concern... Is the Church helping or hindering the true gospel which includes repentance of sin? Are we, as the Church, looking for loopholes or twisting Scripture and its context to suit our personal desires – ultimately, to enable us to fit in with the society around us? With this in mind, I would caution the Church against fulfilling Paul's references to 'itching ears,' evident in 2 Timothy 4:1-5 (NIV):

> *In the presence of God and of Christ Jesus, who will judge the living and the dead, and in view of his appearing and his kingdom, I give you this charge: Preach the word; be prepared in season and out of season; correct, rebuke and encourage—with great patience and careful instruction. For the time will come when people will not put up with sound*

doctrine. Instead, to suit their own desires, they will gather around them a great number of teachers to say what their itching ears want to hear. They will turn their ears away from the truth and turn aside to myths. But you, keep your head in all situations, endure hardship, do the work of an evangelist, discharge all the duties of your ministry.

It helps us to consider this as we return to our main question, asking what it is that Paul's teachings reveal on the subject of same-sex relationships, sexuality and holiness.

WHAT DOES THE APOSTLE PAUL SAY ABOUT SEXUALITY AND SAME-SEX RELATIONSHIPS?

Sexual orientation is not sinful

Romans 1 (quoted earlier in this chapter) is probably the most important passage of Scripture in this discussion. Before we unpack it in depth, it's important both to acknowledge and to understand that we all have sinful desires and *having same-sex desires is not a sin.*

Think about it, I am a heterosexual married man... Does that automatically mean I don't notice a beautiful woman other than my wife? Of course not. Is it a sin to notice her? No! However, what I do *after* I have noticed her can become a sin – it's called giving in to temptation. If I look for longer (what I mean by this is to not remove my eyes from the person after that first glance), think about her longer than I should, choose to undress her in my mind, or even picture myself sexually with her, all of this in God's eyes, would be sinful behaviour and driven by lust.

During His ministry years, Jesus clearly addressed this issue of lust in the Sermon on the Mount saying:

You have heard that it was said, "You shall not commit adultery." But I tell you that anyone who looks at a woman lustfully has already committed adultery with her in his heart. (Matthew 5:27-28, NIV)

Here, Jesus teaches that looking at a woman is not the key issue at stake. Just as money itself is not the root of all evil but rather the desire and lust *for* money is (1 Timothy 6:10), so Jesus demonstrates that lust is a mental condition; one that starts intentionally, in the heart and the mind. Looking lustfully at another person is a choice and a sin which can lead to entanglement - something that King David discovered through his sexual affair with Bathsheba (2 Samuel 11).

In the same way, if someone experiences same-sex attractions and notices good-looking people around them but chooses deliberately *not* to act upon it or to look for longer, then they have not given way to the temptation of lust and not been sinful in their behaviour.

And there's better news... For those like me who may struggle sometimes in looking for too long, there's the awesome opportunity to ask for forgiveness, set about changing our attitude and know that God *has* forgiven us. In fact, the Bible says, that our sin is thrown away from us as far as the east is from the west (Psalm 103:12)!

So, to be clear, our sexual orientations are not what make us sinful, it is what we do with them and whether we intentionally practise and act upon our sexual desires. In fact, this is one of the debates around Romans 1.

When Paul says in Romans 1:26, 'Because of this, God gave them over to shameful lusts. Even their women exchanged natural sexual relations for unnatural ones,' it raises the question of what Paul means by 'shameful lusts' (NIV) also translated as 'dishonourable passions' (ESV). The word in the Greek is '*pathos*' and is only used twice elsewhere in the New Testament (my emphasis added to denote the correct word):

> *Put to death, therefore, whatever belongs to your earthly nature: sexual immorality, impurity, **lust**, evil desires and greed, which is idolatry.*

> (Colossians 3:5, NIV)

> *That each of you should learn to control your own body in a way that is holy and honourable, not in **passionate** lust like the pagans, who do not know God; and that in this matter no one should wrong or take advantage of a brother or sister. The Lord will punish all those who commit such sins, as we told you and warned you before.*

> (1 Thessalonians 4:5, NIV)

On both occasions in these passages, Paul uses the word '*pathos*' to warn against sexual excess or lust. Paul seems to be warning against allowing one's sexual desires to boil over, rather than rebuking individuals for having a sexual desire or sexual orientation at all.[31] This initial statement from Paul is not reserved for those of same-sex attraction alone, but for heterosexuals also.

Paul's words therefore confirm what we have already stated that it is not a sin to notice an attractive person, but that all people, regardless of orientation, have a responsibility to keep their passions under control, in line with the fruit of the Spirit of self-control (Galatians 5). Therefore, it would seem reasonable to affirm that same-sex orientation is not the sin; rather, what the individual decides to do with his or her desires *is*, and this equally applies to those professing to be heterosexual.

All sexual sin is sin

Let me be completely clear so there is no scope for misunderstanding my words.

It is so important that we don't put same-sex practice on a sinful scale of its own; if a person of heterosexual orientation has sex before marriage, sleeps around and fails to keep their dishonouring passions in check, we must not overlook the fact that in the eyes of God, they are equally sinful and in need of forgiveness, through true repentance.

Is this point important?

Absolutely!

There has been substantial damage inflicted on those who experience same-sex attractions by the idea that because their sexual orientation is not deemed acceptable by their family or peers, or particularly the Christian community, they should condemn themselves and end up hiding, hating themselves, self-harming or even worse.

How tragic and how awful!

By lovingly helping the same-sex community understand that all excessive, misplaced sexual desire is equally sinful, therefore not excluding heterosexuals from this call to godly behaviour, it sends a message that we are all in this *together*; that, as God's people, we are *all* called to self-denial and sexual restraint.

We must not forget nor underestimate that alongside those struggling with same-sex preferences, there are plenty of heterosexual Christian individuals, likewise struggling with similar, excessive lust. Not one of us is exempt from the impact of Paul's words – which, don't forget, are inspired by God and literally, 'God-breathed'.

The key is that our human frailty in this gives us an opportunity to recognise that *we are all struggling* and in our common struggle can help one another in our journeys for the Lord!

So, let's clarify: Is Paul saying practising same-sex relationships is a sin?

I agree, it's really key that we get to the bottom of this question so there is no scope for misunderstanding God's Word on this matter of LGBTQ+.

Whilst we've discussed above that we are all capable of lusting sexually after others, in Romans 1:26-27, Paul particularly addresses the boiling of lust or dishonouring passions, saying that there has been an exchange of 'natural' heterosexual sexual relationships for 'unnatural' same-sex relationships:[32]

Because of this, God gave them over to shameful lusts. Even their women exchanged natural sexual relations for unnatural ones. In the same way the men also abandoned natural relations with women and were inflamed with lust for one another. Men committed shameful acts with other men and received in themselves the due penalty for their error. (NIV)

Whilst having the desires and not acting on them is commendable (something, we noted in earlier chapters when Jesus encourages celibacy in Matthew 19), Paul's words here seem to indicate that the practice of same-sex relationships is a deviation from God's intended, 'natural' heterosexual design described in Genesis. Therefore, in this vein, the pursuit of same-sex sexual relationships is considered sinful by Paul.

Also, it is worth noting that Paul addresses same-sex relationships or homosexuality in other areas, such as 1 Timothy and 1 Corinthians (shown below):

We also know that the law is made not for the righteous but for lawbreakers and rebels, the ungodly and sinful, the unholy and irreligious, for those who kill their fathers or mothers, for murderers, for the sexually immoral, for those practicing homosexuality, for slave traders and liars and perjurers— and for whatever else is contrary to the sound doctrine.

(1 Timothy 1:9-10, NIV)

Or do you not know that wrongdoers will not inherit the kingdom of God? Do not be deceived. Neither the sexually immoral nor idolaters nor adulterers, nor men who have sex with men, nor thieves, nor the greedy, nor drunkards, nor slanderers, nor swindlers will inherit the kingdom of God. And that is what some of you were. But you were washed, you were sanctified, you were justified in the name of the Lord Jesus Christ and by the Spirit of our God.

(1 Corinthians 6:9, NIV)

Some have tried to write these passages out of the debate by arguing that Paul is not referring to consensual same-sex relationships.[33] There is a new popular argument that states same-sex consenting relationships weren't around in the 1st century AD and that Paul is referring here to something distinct; to relationships where an old man has intercourse with a younger man, perhaps even prostitution, but not individuals involved in a consenting, loving relationship. This view has gained traction and comes up increasingly in conversations, particularly with those who read the Bible rarely or haven't studied it in depth. It's certainly a very convenient argument to affirm same-sex relationships.

However, among many scholars of affirming and non-affirming stances, this understanding is not accepted.[34] There is plenty of proof documented by ancient historians that same-sex relationships *did* exist in the 1st century AD and most would agree that Paul is speaking here, against homosexual practice - whether consenting or not, and whether loving or not.[35]

It is very hard to deny that Paul is speaking against same-sex sexual intercourse, when he refers to 'men who practise homosexuality' in 1 Corinthians 6:9 and 1 Timothy 1:10. Even in the Septuagint translation of Leviticus 18:22 and 20:13 the same Greek words are used: *'arsenokoitai'* which combines the words *'arsen'* (male) and *'koite'* (bed) – a combination which demonstrates that Paul is directly addressing the act of sexual activity between two men. The fact Paul uses these same words in relation to homosexuality, gives credence to claims that Paul is deliberately upholding the Holiness Code of Leviticus beyond the cross, even though we are under grace and not under law. This further demonstrates that God's holy character and His requirements concerning human sexuality in the Law *still count today*; they have never changed.

A NOTE OF CHALLENGE...

However, there is a twist in the Romans passage that all conservative Christians need to take to heart. Paul appears to paint a clear picture of homosexual practice as being sinful, yet it can be easy to miss what Paul says in Romans 2:1 (NIV):

You, therefore, have no excuse, you who pass judgment on someone else, for at whatever point you judge another, you are condemning yourself, because you who pass judgment do the same things.

Paul seems to take the weapon of judgment aimed at those practising same-sex relationships and turns it on those wielding it; on those who seem keen to point out the sins of others, as if they themselves were faultless. Yet, Paul does not mince his words, pointing out that such people are self-righteous and equally capable of committing sinful acts that grieve God. He states unequivocally, 'you who pass judgment do the same things.'

This is of profound importance to someone like me who, in writing this book on this topic, can so easily spend my time defending the conservative theological cause, yet fail to examine myself.

What about you, as a reader?

Do you passionately fight for traditional biblical relationships whilst lusting after those of the opposite sex?

Do you have pornography issues?

Masturbation issues?

Are you unfaithful to your spouse either physically, emotionally or in your mind?

Then, take Paul's words to heart and don't overlook the sobering fact that, '...at whatever point you judge another, you are condemning yourself' (Romans 2:1, NIV).

Perhaps, we all have work to do? Wouldn't we all like a little grace to be extended towards us in these struggles? Well, in that case, we must start by extending that same grace to individuals of the LGBTQ+ community, whilst still honouring and upholding the Word of God.

So, how can we do this?

The truth is, holding to Scripture whilst still showing love to those who may not agree with it, *is* honouring Scripture.

Same-sex practice is clearly and undeniably a sin in Scripture, contrary to the way the world and many churches are painting the picture.

So, the question is three-fold.

Are we willing to accept that in God's eyes and according to His Holy Word, any sexual relationship outside of that between one male and one female is a sin?

How can we show love and grace to our brothers and sisters in the LGBTQ+ community whilst staying true to God's instruction?

What do we need to do *in our own lives* to ensure that we are not, in fact, hypocrites?

What an incredibly sensitive debate this is! How hard it must be to be all for Jesus, yet find your sexual desires don't line up with His will for your life.

We must all, as God's people, be passionately ready to walk with and support anyone and everyone who faces this reality and struggle. Even for those who may refuse to accept this understanding of Scripture – we must hold out love; we must continue to love them whilst not giving them any false hope.

7

Fill the earth!

SPEAKING REALLY CLEARLY!

Some years ago, I went to visit my friend Steve. Upon arrival, he told me his father-in-law was staying with him. Knowing what I am like, Steve pleaded with me; "Please don't tell him you're a pastor, Mike. He's had a terrible experience with church ministers and will likely get very upset..." I told Steve I couldn't lie but assured him I would not open up conversation about my role in the Church intentionally when speaking with his father-in-law.

So, all good then? Not quite! What do you think his father-in-law's first question was?

Yep, you've guessed it.

"So, Mike, what do you do for a living?"

I reasoned internally for a few moments – along the lines of words like these... *It's not my fault he's had a bad experience with church, and I certainly won't be denying Jesus.* Then, I opened my mouth to speak and muttered nervously, "I'm... I'm a, er, pastor."

What happened next shocked the life out of me! Steve's father-in-law seemed very excited at my words: "Oh wonderful," he said. "Every household needs one of those! In fact, I could do with you coming over to my house in France, I have a number of things for you to attend to."

At this point I was feeling very smug. I thought to myself, *Eat that, Steve. When you're good at evangelism, God opens any door. Now, how shall I walk through this wide-open opportunity?*

Suddenly, Steve jumped into the conversation, "Want a cup of tea, MIKE!"

Of course, in such moments of triumph, there is always time for a cup of tea, right? So off Steve trotted, with what I thought was a tail between his faithless legs, whilst I sat indulging in conversation with my new-found enquirer... or so I thought.

Suddenly, out of the corner of my eye, I noticed my phone flash up with a message from Steve in the kitchen. *Now, what's that doughnut texting me from the kitchen for?* I thought to myself. *I'd better check it in case it's important, whilst trying not to look rude in front of the father-in-law, of course.*

I will never forget the sinking feeling in my heart when I read that text message:

"HE THINKS YOU'RE A PLASTERER!"

My unseen thoughts looked something like this:

"YOU'VE *GOT* TO BE KIDDING ME!"

I must be honest with you, reader. I have *never* vacated a conversation so quickly; that cup of tea ran down my throat like Niagara Falls on a rainy day!

Alongside being hugely embarrassed, I did take away something helpful from that experience. I learned that we need to speak clearly, (in my case, really clearly) as Christians.

Likewise, we need to be clear about what we believe.

It's a sad reality that many Christians, whether affirming or not when it comes to the LGBTQ+ debate, have no idea what the Bible actually says on the matter. Usually, people fall into one of two scenarios: either affirming it simply because they want to go with the flow of current culture around them, or not affirming it because it doesn't fit with their traditional worldview and teaching of Scripture.

Something else I've noticed is that both sides of the fence generally don't like to ask deeper questions about the implications of what it means if we just throw open the doors of the Church to any new sexual practice or expression of sexuality.

Either way, it seems that you can't win... If you oppose the LGBTQ+ movement, you get abused by people in and outside the Church. On the other hand, if you support the movement, then you get abused by those in the Church who maintain a conservative view.

I believe we need to explore what the Bible actually says concerning LGBTQ+ and sexuality; we need to consider the context in which the relevant scriptures were written and ask deep questions, specifically about the implications concerning God's commands to His people on the earth today.

This is the key to ensuring we can be clear with people about who we are and where we choose to stand on the big issues of the day.

THE GENESIS BLUEPRINT

God has been clear with His people from the very beginning in the Bible. There should be no confusion about what God has commanded us to do and no justifiable excuses for our claiming to have misheard Him... He certainly isn't a plasterer; He is our Creator – the one who has given us clear instructions about our identity and our purpose.

It's true that the story of Creation is often ignored when it comes to debates such as this one. But I am struck by the fact that it is within the book of Genesis that we get the answers to many of the world's issues. Let us not forget that this is where the problem between humans and their God began. Satan came into the garden and disrupted God's relationship with His creation, in particular with man and with woman, made in God's image (Genesis 3).

For me, there are two things that stand out within God's Creation account which can speak directly into this matter of sexuality and same-sex relationships. The first is that God created a sacred, ordained order for creation which included man and woman, 'male and female' (Genesis 1:27, NIV). The second is the heart-warming moment in Genesis after God created the earth and everything in it, where He takes a moment to pause and admire it all. The Bible says, 'God saw all that he had made, and it was very good' (Genesis 1:31, NIV).

So, how can we see what constitutes God's good, created order?

I suggest we look at the fruit produced by it.

When a man and a woman come together in physical union, children are the direct result and stand as clear evidence of the blueprint God intended when He commanded humans to multiply and fill the earth (Genesis 1:28). Procreation, literally producing children, does not and cannot happen outside of a relationship between a man and a woman and in the Bible is repeatedly seen as a sign of God's blessing and favour upon the parents who conceived them (1 Samuel 2:21).

The only occasion in the Bible where the conception of children does not involve the direct genetic makeup of one man and one woman is in the Incarnation, when Mary conceives a baby by the power of the Holy Spirit and nine months later gives birth to Jesus Christ. (It is important to briefly acknowledge this, but the scope of my book means we will not explore it further.)

Back to Genesis...

Not once in God's Creation account nor throughout the whole Bible does He affirm same-sex relationships or anything other than heterosexual relationships between two distinct genders of male and female.

It is only when God's creative order is disrupted and humans are compelled to leave His presence, that we see the snowball effect of sin – leading over many years to the present age where sadly, God's created order is not only questioned and rejected; often, it is ridiculed.

When Leviticus 20:13 says a man shall not lie with another man as he does with a woman, it would appear on the basis of the Creation account, to be *more* than a law. As we've explored previously, not only does it comprise part of God's Holiness Code, but it also reveals God's desire for His world and is in line with His created order, which He called 'good', and then blessed with multiplication. In case you have forgotten, you may want to revisit the earlier chapter on 'A good thing the Law counts for nothing, right?'

However, there is one caveat... Whilst Leviticus 20:13 reveals God's heart towards what His Word terms unnatural relationships, the punishment of death is obviously not for our time. This is because, excluding the Holiness Code written on our hearts, we are not under the Law and, what's more, Jesus suffered the punishment for sin on the cross.

Yet, this does not mean we may go ahead in the wake of His death and carry out the acts which are deemed sinful by God's Word and which Jesus died for. Surely, to do this would be to insult Jesus and His sacrifice; tantamount to doing what Hebrews 6:6 terms, 'crucifying the Son of God all over again and subjecting him to public disgrace' (NIV).

Furthermore, if Jesus is rejected and repentance does not occur, the Bible is clear that there will be a day of judgment for all sins when He returns (2 Corinthians 5:10). Our prayer should be that all come to the knowledge and understanding of God and turn from those ways which are offensive to God, and the very reason for which Jesus had to suffer and die.

HOW IMPORTANT IS MULTIPLYING ON THE EARTH?

Let's look once more at Genesis 1:28 (NIV) and God's command to fill the earth:

> *God blessed them and said to them, "Be fruitful and increase in number; fill the earth and subdue it. Rule over the fish in the sea and the birds in the sky and over every living creature that moves on the ground."*

Do we ever take the time to think more deeply about the implications of rejecting this command of God to multiply on the earth?

Is it really that important?

Does God really care about it?

Let's pose some hypothetical questions to consider possible scenarios and how they might impact our thinking when it comes to the LGBTQ+ debate... This is not to say I have the answers, just that I think it is worth exploring whether rejecting God's blueprint for procreation really does have implications.

First off, I wonder...

What would have happened if Adam and Eve had decided to go against God's command to multiply?

Imagine how God would have responded had the conversation gone something like this...

Adam: "Um God, so I need to be up front with you. Eve and I have been talking, and we've decided that actually, we're not really that into each other. I don't think I do fancy her, you see, and well, this might upset You, but I don't think we're going to fill the earth... If that's OK by You?"

Comic though this may seem, it's important to pose the hypothetical scenario for the purposes of our discussion.

Would God have been OK with this? How important to God is the instruction to fill the earth?

Now, let's take it a bit deeper...

Given the increasing presence of LGBTQ+ today, it would be fair to say that our modern society appears to have an agenda in pushing for total acceptance of same-sex relationships, sex changes and various other types of gender dysphoria. Over the years this has impacted a minority of people, but today the number is increasing at a quickening rate (something we will explore further in subsequent chapters).

It seems that many in the Church are up for embracing wholeheartedly the phenomena above on the basis that surely, such things are OK because they're only affecting a minority. But what if that changed, and here come the next hypothetical questions which form in my mind:

What would happen if the whole world decided to come out as homosexual and reject any heterosexual representation of sexuality? What if no more children were conceived or produced? Wouldn't this mean that God's command to multiply had gone bust?

Let's pose another set of questions:

Would it be sinful to reject God's instruction? And, if it would be a sin to reject God's instruction as an entire world of individuals choosing not to embrace God's heterosexual blueprint, does that mean it is a different story if it is only a minority?

Does number play a role in determining whether something is sinful in God's eyes? Do we get to decide for ourselves?

Now, don't get me wrong, I still agree that we should have compassion on the minority for whom these issues are relevant. However, alongside compassion, I want to ask, is it right that we accept the particular agenda the world seems to be advocating? To literally flood every sphere of society with what seems to be akin to indoctrination (in our schools, in our businesses, in our institutions etc), pushing us not only to tolerate and embrace the LGBTQ+ movement but to join in pushing the agenda ourselves?

On the basis of this breadth of influence, it seems fair to question whether the movement has got a little out of control. And, as Christians seeking to apply God's Word to our lives, I can't overemphasise how important it is that we keep asking questions, pray, seek God's Word – and don't just get caught up with the flow of the world when it runs contrary to what we understand as God's instruction.

WHAT ABOUT FAMILY LINES?

Another question I have been pondering recently is the effect of the increasing number of people who seem to be 'coming out' or changing their gender. It was a phenomenon hardly heard of a few years ago, but today I seem to encounter more and more Christians whose children have either come out as homosexual or bisexual or chosen to become non-binary.

Recently, a parent approached me and asked for advice on what secondary school she might choose for her child. She said she was surprised to find that the local school had a room dedicated to LGBTQ+ Pride and another room filled with paintings of drag queens.

Another parent also approached me for advice, this time regarding her autistic daughter's confusion when a boy was allowed to change for P.E. with the girls – as he claims he wants to be a girl... he is just seven years old.

On yet another occasion, I was asked whether a parent should complain to the school after they hosted a 'Kings and Queens Day' and the rather effeminate male teacher decided to wear a dress. Not surprisingly, this confused the child in question.

Let's consider the evidence... Unfortunately, stories like these are just the tip of the iceberg.

It seems that the world is no longer just following a policy of tolerance towards this movement; it is proactively marketing a new alternative to God's creative order.

Has anyone sat down and asked what implications this might have on future generations?

I mean, I understand that some individuals are born with same-sex orientation or gender dysphoria but why are we seeing such an increase? Surely, the rate of people born with sexual orientation other than heterosexual doesn't suddenly jump, because there is something in the water. Could it actually be a direct result of this increasing presence of LGBTQ+ in our twenty-first century; the apparent 'agenda' evident in schools, on social media, in sport, and pretty much everywhere and everything, that is causing such a rise?

I wonder...

So, here comes the next hypothetical question playing on my mind:

If there continues to be an increase in people choosing same-sex relationships and gender changes, what effect could this have on future generational family lines?

People who ordinarily would have married someone of the opposite gender and had children, may now choose not to. So, surely, that spells the end of their family line? Sounds a bit far-fetched, maybe, but could this be a form of spiritual confusion in our modern day? To confuse many individuals and prevent them from fulfilling God's original blueprint instruction to multiply on the earth and continue family lines – and the line of humanity? That's a lot of people not to be born nor given the chance to choose salvation.

Now, deep down, I know God is much bigger than that and knows all things and will work all things for good in the end for those who love Him (Romans 8:28). However, should we not at least be pondering these questions prayerfully?

Let's not underestimate how important humanity is to God and how the Bible throughout is meticulous in noting down genealogies and family lines.

IDENTITY AND THE IMAGE OF GOD

Building a little further on the idea of whether there is a spiritual agenda behind the LGBTQ+ movement in our days, I have one more question to pose, this time not hypothetical but important even so:

Have we considered how God feels about our choosing to identify neither as male nor female?

After all, we are made in God's image.

What's more, the Bible talks about knitting us together in our mother's womb (Jeremiah 1:5) and there are many instances where God names those whom He calls in the Bible (Genesis 17:5, Genesis 17:19, Genesis 32:22-32, Luke 1:13). This suggests He has a plan for who He created each one of us to be with unique genetic makeup, and this includes our sexual orientation. Therefore, is it right for us to reject His wisdom?

I was discussing this question with a family member recently, and they asked me how I would view someone born with a missing chromosome. Usually, human cells have forty-six chromosomes in twenty-three pairs, half given by the father and half by the mother at conception.[36] Some people, however, are born with chromosomes missing or even extra chromosomes, for instance forty-five or forty-seven rather than forty-six. It is believed by some scientists that this can result in health issues and have an impact on sexuality and sexual orientation.[37]

Having pondered this question, I realised that the only answer I can give is that we all need to be gracious. Sexuality and our individual sexual orientation may or may not be biologically determined (the arguments on this one continue to be debated by scientists and scholars alike). However, as we have seen in this book, the greater question remains...

What will we sacrifice for kingdom-living?

If indeed same-sex relationships, or any relationship for that matter, are deemed outside of the will of God for our lives, would we be willing to give them up for the sake of kingdom-living? Or are we saying, we will only accept God on *our* terms?

Regardless of the answer each of us gives to this question, we all need to show one another grace; as we are called, not to judge one another, but to love one another (Colossians 3:12-14)!

The fact is, since the Fall of mankind, we are all born not quite as God originally intended.

Since rejecting God, we have all lost our identity in God's original blueprint.

We all need to show love and compassion to one another whilst exploring who it is God has created each one of us to be, working out how to honour His original blueprint and encouraging one another towards pursuing our identity in Christ.

I am certain that all of us have struggles to different degrees with different things. However, no matter the struggle, all of us need to be presented with the gospel and the kingdom of God. Our role as believers is to present that gospel by showing individuals who may be struggling that they have a choice; they can make a decision to lay down their current life choices, accept Jesus' gift of salvation and embrace being made into a new creation in Christ Jesus. After all, this is our new identity and means the idol of the life we once knew is to be put to death in favour of the life in the Spirit that Jesus bids us to take on.

All this, knowing that our time on earth is short, the eternal life we will inherit does not include our sexuality (in Matthew 22:30, Jesus remarks that there will be no marriage in heaven, and we will be like the angels who do not possess sexuality as such), and lust will not be what drives us. It is also worth noting that in Matthew 19:12, Jesus says some are born eunuchs – what significance does this have on the discussion of gender? Whilst the LGBTQ+ movement puts all sexuality and gender together as one, I believe the discussion of same sex practice and gender identification may warrant being seen as separate discussions. Either way, we need much grace as we are dealing with precious people who are dealing with big life questions.

So, accepting people may be born with their struggles, we still point them to their true identity in Christ and celebrate that when God made humans, He made us in His image - what an honour! I have no doubt that the devil would love us to eradicate the male or female in us altogether as this would serve to eradicate the very image of God in us.

A NOTE OF ENCOURAGEMENT...

That said, I want to be clear.

This book is not about demonising or condemning the LGTBQ+ community! Remember, Jesus calls us to keep love at the forefront of all our interactions with every individual. So, we must remember also that if there *is* a spiritual agenda behind the movement, then it is possible that the individuals caught up within the movement are like pawns, unwittingly caught up in a spiritual battle.

As a man who loves his films, I find the premise of *The Matrix* interesting to consider here, as one possible representation of what it is like to be caught up within something unwittingly.

Mike Williams

But I digress...

What I wish to emphasise is this: Let's not heap pressure on the amazing individuals in our communities around us who are genuinely struggling and questioning their sexuality; but let's seek to come alongside them, invite them to share their struggles, treat them with compassion, respect and with love - and always point them to Jesus.

It's important to ask the questions in this book and it is vital to understand what the Bible says on the subject, but even more important is that *we point individuals to Jesus*.

He is the one who knows them best and knows every inch of their struggle and He is the one who can invite them by the power of His Holy Spirit to take the leap; to become a new creation and, as is true for all of us in Christ, to continue to walk out their salvation with '[godly] fear and with trembling...' (Philippians 2:12, NIV).

Not forgetting Sodom and Gomorrah

WHAT REALLY HAPPENED?

The Genesis account

I think it would be remiss of me not to mention Sodom and Gomorrah when dealing with the topic of sexuality and same-sex relationships.

Genesis 19 tells us that God rained down fire and sulphur on the cities because of their wickedness (v.24). Prior to this devasting punishment, the Bible records an incident of what appears to be intentional sexual exploitation. But what *actually* happened?

You can read the full story in Genesis 19:1-11.

The men of the cities of Sodom and Gomorrah catch news of male guests, staying at the house of Lot. They come to the door of Lot's house in substantial numbers and the Bible describes it like this:

**All the men from every part of Sodom and Gomorrah –
both young and old** – *surrounded the house. They called
to Lot, 'Where are the men who came to you tonight? Bring
them out to us so that we can have sex with them.'*

(Genesis 19:4-5, NIV, my emphasis added)

There is something extraordinary in the story, however; the men of Sodom are unaware that the two men staying under Lot's roof happen to be angels, sent by God.

In response to the Sodomite men, Lot remonstrates with them and, in an effort to protect the angels and deter the men from their objective which he calls 'a wicked thing' (v.7), Lot offers up his daughters instead.

What happens next is supernatural as the angels intervene. They remove Lot from the clamour of the angry men and blind every single one of them. Then, they instruct Lot and his family to leave the cities immediately, explaining that God's punishment is imminent.

What a story!

It must be acknowledged that many scholars have rejected claims that the account in Genesis 19 has any bearing on our discussion of same-sex relationships and whether God affirms them. Let's explore why...

In their view, there are two key points to raise.

Firstly, they believe that the reason Lot acted as he did was about *hospitality;* he wanted to prevent the men from making what would have been a terrible mistake - as failing to show hospitality to guests would have gone against his understanding of a cultural mandate. This is something Waldemar Janzen describes at length in his book *Old Testament*

Ethics where, for Janzen, there is a running theme of hospitality evident In the narrative of the Old Testament which he calls 'familial paradigm'.[38] Janzen calls the components which make up familial paradigm in the Old Testament, 'life, land, and hospitality', which collectively demonstrate God's will and God's Law lived out as a narrative.[39]

It is true that only one chapter prior to the Sodom and Gomorrah account, we see Abraham bow down to three visitors from the Lord who announce the judgment to come on Sodom and Gomorrah (Genesis 18:1-8). Abraham's response to their visit is to bow down and plead with them to allow him to bring water and refresh them, thereby showing hospitality and proving its cultural importance. In this vein, it is probable that for Lot, the act of extending hospitality would have had similar significance.

Interestingly, the story of Sodom and Gomorrah (Genesis 19) is similar to that of Judges 19 where a Levite priest and his concubine are shown hospitality by an old man from Gibeah. As occurs in the Sodom and Gomorrah story, the men of the city want to 'have sex' with the Levite priest (Genesis 19:22), but the old man is incensed by this 'wicked' request and offers up his virgin daughter and the priest's concubine. Is this act of offering his daughter and the concubine another act of preserving the ethos of hospitality towards the priest? Ultimately, in the case of Judges 19, we cannot be sure, but the parallels to the Sodom and Gomorrah story are noticeable.

On this basis, I can concede that Lot's actions to prevent the men from having sex with his two male visitors may have been motivated by a desire to preserve the cultural mandate of hospitality. However, we cannot overlook the biblical record which reveals that divine judgment for the sins of the cities of Sodom and Gomorrah is determined *prior* to this incident.

As we mentioned previously, in Genesis 18, angels visit Abraham and as they depart, the Lord warns him of the impending disaster, stating that 'the outcry against Sodom and Gomorrah is so great and their sin is so grievous' (v.20). So, punishment for the full extent of their sin is declared *before* the recorded incident of Genesis 19, *before* the men of Sodom and Gomorrah had failed to show hospitality to the angels with their proposal of homosexual exploitation... *not after.*

A second key thing that scholars claim about this passage is that the sexual sin itself was about an incident of *gang rape,* not consensual same-sex sexual relationships.[40]

The question is, are the scholars right in their interpretation of this passage and the motivations of the people featured within it?

Does this passage have no bearing on our discussion of God, sexuality and same-sex relationships?

I'm not sure that I agree fully with scholars on this, and I shall explain why...

Yes, this does appear to be an incident of appalling intentional gang rape. Making reference to 'all the men' of Sodom and Gomorrah both 'young and old' (Genesis 19:4, NIV), the Bible indicates a substantial volume of men is involved. And, as I explained with regards to Lot and his motivations above, this sexual exploitation would undoubtedly transgress the code of treating guests with flawless hospitality. However, I do believe this event does also reveal something of God's attitude towards same-sex relationships.

Other biblical references to Sodom and Gomorrah

It is helpful on this count to consider other references to Sodom and Gomorrah contained within the biblical record.

Firstly, in **Ezekiel**, the voice of God refers to the sinfulness of Sodom and Gomorrah, yet it seems as though sexual sin is not mentioned:

> "Not only did you walk in their ways and do according to their abominations; within a very little time you were more corrupt than they in all your ways. As I live," declares the Lord GOD, "your sister Sodom and her daughters have not done as you and your daughters have done. Behold, this was the guilt of your sister Sodom: she and her daughters had pride, excess of food, and prosperous ease, but did not aid the poor and needy. They were haughty and did an abomination before me. So, I removed them, when I saw it."

> (Ezekiel 16:47-50, NIV)

I wonder, could there be more here than first meets the eye?

As Kevin DeYoung rightly points out, verses 47 and 50 speak of 'abominations', which is translated from the Hebrew word 'ebah'. It is important to highlight the fact that this same word 'ebah' occurs in Leviticus 18:22 and 20:13 – verses which we acknowledged earlier in this book constitute the Holiness Code of the Old Testament Law prohibiting same-sex sexual relationships.[41] I would suggest therefore that the use of the same word in each of these distinct passages gives us reason to pause.

DeYoung also points out:

> Literature from the second temple Judaism (the time between 516 BC and the final destruction of the temple in 70 AD) shows that Sodom's reputation for same-sex behaviour cannot be explained as a first-century invention by Philo or Josephus.[42]

Then, if we read **Jude**, we see a picture of Sodom and Gomorrah as a city punished for sexual sin and unnatural desires:

> *In a similar way, Sodom and Gomorrah and the*
> *surrounding towns gave themselves up to sexual*
> *immorality and perversion. They serve as an example*
> *of those who suffer the punishment of eternal fire.*

(Jude 7, NIV)

This reference to the giving up of themselves to sexual immorality and perversion lines up with what Paul calls 'the exchanging of natural sexual relations for unnatural ones' in Romans 1:26 (NIV).

For these reasons stated above, whilst I have chosen not to focus too much on Sodom and Gomorrah, I do believe that scholars are mistaken in considering Genesis 19 to have no bearing on whether God does affirm same-sex relationships.

I think the collective references to Sodom and Gomorrah found in both the Old and New Testament demonstrate that, at the very least, there is no positive view shown here, of same-sex relationships.

Furthermore, if considered in terms of the word, '*ebah*' as an 'abomination' in God's eyes, we *cannot* biblically affirm them.

PART 3
PRACTISING LOVE AND TRUTH IN TANDEM

9

Kingdom over culture

A CHOICE TO MAKE

One of the great questions I'm asked when discussing the same-sex topic is: "What are you suggesting a homosexual Christian *does* with their desires?"

We've already looked at what the Bible says on this issue, in terms of our being prepared to turn our back on sexual lust outside of heterosexual marriage, but this is a really important question to consider.

It's so easy to tell people what Scripture says on the topic of sexuality, but it's a lot harder to encourage them to follow it through, once they realise choosing Jesus may mean they will have to consider remaining single. I'm acutely aware that it's so much easier for me, being married and heterosexual, to readily write about these challenges than it is for those who may actually be facing them due to their own struggle with same-sex attraction.

In this chapter, we will explore fully what Scripture is asking someone with same sex-attraction to do and why.

Let's start with the words we looked at earlier when Jesus was speaking on marriage as it was in the beginning. In Matthew 19:12, Jesus says, 'some choose to be eunuchs for the sake of the kingdom' (NIV).

As I have said previously, the parable of the Precious Pearl tells the story of a man who gave up everything for the kingdom of God (Matthew 13:45-46). This is the type of disciple that Jesus requires; someone who will literally sell all that they have and stop at nothing to gain Him, the most precious treasure of all. A follower who will put down their 'fishing nets' (their businesses or old way of life), be prepared to leave their home and family if required, and even contemplate dying for the kingdom's sake.

This is the kingdom-choice we are faced with:

Choosing God's kingdom over the culture around us.

This is not a call given to us by a demanding God who wants to control us yet has no understanding of the pain that this may cause us. No, for each of us who choose to follow Jesus, this call is given by a God who personally identifies with us on every front.

A God who... *personally* came to earth, subjected Himself to the same temptations and pressures we face, and submitted Himself to His Father's will to die a barbaric death on a cross...

All in order to pay *personally* for the sin of those who denied and hated Him, of those who made themselves His enemies.

People like you and people like me.

A CHALLENGE TO THE CHURCH

I find it alarming that in many cases, the Modern Church appears to have lost its understanding of the mission of God. Whilst those belonging to the Early Church in Acts fearlessly preached the gospel in public squares and regularly faced the realities of arrest and, worse, the ever-present threat of excruciating martyrdom, most of us in the Modern Church know nothing of these things (see Acts 8:1). In fact, I think it would be fair to say that Modern Christianity in our western society seems tame in contrast.

I wonder if you would agree with me if I said that the Modern Church seems more concerned about the fringe issues than it does about the key issue; prioritising the style of worship, room-lighting preferences or the brand of coffee above the call of the Great Commission to reach out beyond the church doors to the lost in the communities around us.

I admit these words may sound harsh, but I think there is a degree of truth in what I am saying here – and I do not consider myself or my own church family to be exempt from this challenge!

I think it boils down to the Modern Church taking on the consumerism of western society; sadly, most Christians who regularly attend church appear to be consumers rather than contributors. Many leave churches today, because they are not happy with what they get – and for some who choose to leave having taken offence at something minor, it is tragic that they go on to lose their faith in Jesus altogether.

Does this sound like a church that understands the call to kingdom-life?

When Jesus spoke of being the bread of life in John 6, declaring that true followers would have to eat and drink of His flesh, many found this a hard teaching:

On hearing it, many of his disciples said, "This is a hard teaching. Who can accept it?"

Aware that his disciples were grumbling about this, Jesus said to them, "Does this offend you? Then what if you see the Son of Man ascend to where he was before! The Spirit gives life; the flesh counts for nothing. The words I have spoken to you—they are full of the Spirit and life. Yet there are some of you who do not believe." For Jesus had known from the beginning which of them did not believe and who would betray him. He went on to say, "This is why I told you that no one can come to me unless the Father has enabled them." From this time many of his disciples turned back and no longer followed him.

"You do not want to leave too, do you?" Jesus asked the Twelve.

Simon Peter answered him, "Lord, to whom shall we go? You have the words of eternal life. We have come to believe and to know that you are the Holy One of God."

(John 6:60-69, NIV)

Do you see the difference between 1st century Christianity and Christianity today? Are we breeding a church like those disciples who found the teaching so hard that they turned away?

Should we be asking one another the same questions that Jesus asked:

"Does this offend you?"

"Are you going to turn away as well?"

I'll be honest, I'm aware that I may come across as a straight-talking black and white preacher, so I suppose I shouldn't be surprised when I encounter opposition. I will concede that some areas of the Bible may seem grey rather than black and white, however it is important to state that this is not the case with the topic of same-sex relationships. Even so, it surprises me just how many Christians there are today who complain when undeniable truth is preached and afterwards, demand an audience with the pastor to state that they are offended. Most of the time, it seems that the problem arises from their lack of respect for God's preachers and unwillingness to accept God's Word on the areas of their lives that they are unwilling to change. This is not choosing the kingdom of God; this is choosing the culture around us and choosing to live comfortably.

We live in a time where we are quick to paint Jesus as the loving, kind, merciful son of God - a representation of Him which is biblically supported. At the same time, we refuse to hold this in balance with the way Jesus describes Himself to His brothers in John 7:7, as one whom the world hates:

> *My time is not yet here; for you any time will do. The world cannot hate you, but it **hates** me because I testify that its works are evil.*

> (NIV, my emphasis added)

Can Jesus possibly be unoffensive to the world when using the statement above? And, what about when we, as Jesus' followers, are part of the equation?

Let's consider what Jesus says in John 15:19 when He tells His disciples how the world views them:

*If you belonged to the world, it would love you as its own.
As it is, you do not belong to the world, but I have chosen
you out of the world. **That is why the world hates you.***

(NIV, my emphasis added)

Clearly, Jesus was hated, and His disciples were hated; can we as the Modern Church today expect anything different?

Can we really expect to be *embraced* by the world?

Choosing the kingdom of God over culture is to deliberately reject the ways of the world, even though our flesh desires the things of the world. It is to sacrifice the desires of the flesh and to lay down what pleases us in favour of the things that please God. That is why Jesus said what He did:

*If anyone would come after me, let him deny himself and
take up his cross and follow me. For whoever would save his
life will lose it, but whoever loses his life for my sake will find
it. For what will it profit a man if he gains the whole world
and forfeits his soul? Or what shall a man give for his soul?*

(Luke 9:23, NIV)

Do you see the kingdom-call here? It is a dangerous one, a painful call, and it requires us to say, "Lord I will lay down whatever it takes to line up with Your kingdom. Even if this means deliberately laying down my expression of sexuality and desires." It is the type of commitment Ruth made to Naomi when she said to the older woman:

*Don't urge me to leave you or to turn back from you.
Where you go, I will go, and where you stay, I will stay.
Your people will be my people and your God my God.*

(Ruth 1:16, NIV)

Now, let's be very honest and ask ourselves as individuals, is there anything we are unwilling to give up for the kingdom-call of God... whether it be money, cars, houses, relationships, or perhaps even our sexuality? Are we willing to surrender it all, denying ourselves and the flesh for the sake of the kingdom?

Consider what we might call all of these things.

The answer is idols... a word that makes us feel very uncomfortable.

But, let's face it, anything that comes before God is classed as an idol – which is exactly how Paul unfolded his teaching on sexuality in Romans 1:21-25 (NIV). It began with idolatry:

> *For although they knew God, they neither glorified him*
> *as God nor gave thanks to him, but their thinking became*
> *futile, and their foolish hearts were darkened. Although they*
> *claimed to be wise, they became fools and exchanged the*
> *glory of the immortal God for images made to look like a*
> *mortal human being and birds and animals and reptiles.*
>
> *Therefore, God gave them over in the sinful desires of*
> *their hearts to sexual impurity for the degrading of their*
> *bodies with one another. They exchanged the truth about*
> *God for a lie and worshipped and served created things*
> *rather than the Creator – who is forever praised. Amen.*

Again, I know this is a hard teaching for each of us to swallow and apply; sadly, it is not one I see being taught clearly or prioritised in churches very often.

Instead, it seems as though many churches wish to prioritise filling their auditoriums and keep people there by making them feel comfortable. However, the truth is that the Word of God should be anything but comfortable to a sinful world!

Churches who favour the depiction of Jesus as a fluffy, loving, meek saviour need to take a reality check: Revelation 19 says that Jesus will soon return, not as a pushover, but as a conquering Saviour and King!

> *[He] treads out the winepress of the fury*
> *of the wrath of God almighty.*

(Revelation 19:15, NIV)

Does that sound fluffy to you?

Now, I'm not seeking to be harsh or to offend people deliberately. Nor am I seeking to be one of those preachers who constantly bangs out heavy 'fire and brimstone' messages. I merely want to bring a balance to the table in this debate; to encourage us to recognise that we risk eradicating any reverence or fear for God when we supplant God with culture and state, adhering to what they say rather than considering God as our first authority.

God loves us.

John 3:16 says, He *so* loves us that He sent His one and only son to die for us. So that, if we believe in Him (including His message of our need for repentance), we will turn, be forgiven and receive eternal life. He came to save us, not only from Satan's influence, but equally importantly, He came to save us from ourselves and our sinful desires. Let's not forget that Satan's sin before God was to wish to supplant Him and since Adam and Eve's rejection of God's instruction brought sin into the line of humanity, every single person has likewise struggled to lay down self and let God be God.

The fact is: We are *called* to die to our inner selves.

We are *called* to lay down our old life.

We are *called* to take up and embrace the kingdom-life.

We must remember what Jesus said to His disciples:

> *No one who puts a hand to the plough and looks back is fit for service in the kingdom of God.*

(Luke 9:62, NIV)

ISN'T THIS CALL IMPOSSIBLE?

So often when I discuss the idea of celibacy with those who affirm same-sex relationships, they respond as though it is our relationships on the earth that define us completely – and this is why many see their sexual orientation as their identity and refuse to surrender it to God.

But haven't they forgotten something?

As Christians, we have the privilege of being God's children, meaning we are citizens of heaven. Just as Jesus said to His disciples, the truth is we are not of this world, neither do we live for this world (John 17:14, 15:19). We are living for the world to come, the kingdom that has no end!

Now, let's think about that for a moment and consider its implications.

First, let's consider things from a temporal perspective. Heaven is *eternal*... But how long is our life on the earth?

Of course, the answer is that we don't know.

True, some individuals have lived to be over 100 years old but generally, few of us make it to that age. I think we can safely conclude therefore, that life on the earth is relatively short.

So, if life is short, and we are being asked to make certain sacrifices in that time, would it be wrong of me to suggest that our relatively short-term sufferings are worthwhile for what will be long-term eternal gain?

I wonder...

You see, often, we like to make out that any sacrifice asked of us by God's Word is abhorrent! We are so quick to exclaim, "But why would a loving God ask me to sacrifice that? I couldn't possibly! That isn't what a loving Father would ask of me, surely?"

Yet, surely, it is nothing compared to the sacrifice He made on the cross.

And let's not forget *why* Jesus endured the cross. The Bible tells us that it was 'for the joy set before him', that He might be reunited with God in heaven and make it possible for all of humanity once more to be with God and experience eternal life (Hebrews 12:2, NIV). I would say the same choice is open to us; just as Jesus did, we can set ourselves to endure short-term earthly sacrifices for long-term eternal gain.

In 1 Peter, the disciple Peter writes of exactly this viewpoint, encouraging the Church of believers to look beyond their current struggles:

> *And after you have suffered a little while, the God of all grace, who has called you to his eternal glory in Christ, will himself restore, confirm, strengthen, and establish you. To him be the dominion forever and ever. Amen.*

> (1 Peter 5:10-11, NIV)

The sufferings of which Peter speaks here, refer to all the temptations we face as believers – which I'm sure today would include all the sexual temptations of excessive lust and sexual relations outside of a heterosexual marriage relationship, also. But look at the reward for a little suffering... 'eternal glory in Christ'! Isn't that brilliant!

Another encouragement we may take from keeping an eternal perspective is that, in fact, Jesus reveals that in heaven, our relationships with others will not define us or give us a sense of our identity.

On one occasion, the Pharisees asked Jesus to determine whose wife a woman would be when she died, given that in her life she had had several husbands. Jesus answered:

> *At the resurrection people will neither marry nor be given in marriage; they will be like the angels in heaven.*

(Matthew 22:30, NIV)

You see what this means?

Jesus' words imply that we won't desire anyone sexually in heaven. That means any short-term hard sacrifice we may choose to make on earth is temporary.

Furthermore, that's why it is so important that we are willing to lay it all down for the kingdom; because by making our identity and earthly purpose about a relationship, a person or our sexuality, is ultimately, to make our earthly life an idol – something God completely detests! In fact, Timothy Keller points out the danger of making our identity about anything in our earthly lives when speaking of the parable Jesus told of the 'Rich man and Lazarus,' saying:

> *In the parable of the Rich Man and Lazarus (Luke 26:19–31) the "rich man" in hell has no name because that was all he*

was—just a rich man. If you make wealth your very identity, and something takes the money away, there is no "you" left.[43]

Whilst Keller is talking about making wealth our identity, this also applies to other earthly matters.

For instance, we had a homeless man in church called Andy, so everyone called him 'homeless Andy' (inappropriately, we now understand). After much perseverance, we convinced the local authorities to house him. This left us with a wonderful revelation... What would we now call homeless Andy? He was no longer homeless! Well, what about calling him 'Andy'?

Our situation, our success, and even our sexuality are not our identities... we have names! God knows us by our names. Therefore, if when we enter heaven, we no longer have a sexual orientation, we will still have an identity. We have names!

A NOTE OF ENCOURAGEMENT...

Unquestionably, this kingdom-life over culture is, as Jesus says, a hard teaching. A life in Christ certainly is a tough calling and does require that effectively, we die to ourselves. Just as Jesus submitted Himself to the Father's will and willingly died on the cross, now we must imitate Him. As Bonhoeffer says:

When Christ calls a man, he bids him come and die.[44]

Bonhoeffer is not talking about physical death here; he is talking about putting to death our will in favour of God the Father's will.

Is it an impossible call to embrace short-term sacrifice for long-term eternal gain?

Is it impossible to choose the kingdom of God over culture?

It certainly would be if we did not also have the incredible help of the Holy Spirit who makes Himself and His supernatural power available to us from the moment we submit our will to God's and choose His Word as our authority on all things... *Even, when it comes to our sexuality.*

In fact, this is surely the power of Christ in us, the hope of glory (Colossians 1:27). One thing we who comprise the Modern Church need to rediscover is the power of the Holy Spirit to transform individuals and empower us to overcome anything which is in opposition to God's instruction for our lives.

I was reminded of this truth recently, when a man in his late twenties approached me after I had preached. He wanted to tell me his testimony of how he had first encountered Jesus. He told me he had been a drug dealer for years and had made a lot of money by it. One evening, he felt overwhelmed by the feeling of disappointment in himself and his life choices to the point of suicidal thoughts. He said, "what happened that night transformed my life."

While suicidal thoughts swam round his mind, he described how "a presence overwhelmed me, and I suddenly felt instructed, not by words but by compulsion to download the Bible onto my phone" - which was odd given that he had no background in Christianity. He then explained how he grabbed large quantities of drugs in his possession and deliberately flushed them all down the toilet. The next day something was noticeably different which he summed up saying, "I no longer had a taste for drugs myself, and I haven't taken drugs for a very long time."

He told me also that at the time it occurred he had no idea who or what the presence was that caused this event. Having since started coming to church, he is now convinced it was the Holy Spirit who not only instructed him to give up the drugs but also provided him with the supernatural power needed to overcome his own addiction.

This, however, did not come without a cost; there were consequences to his actions that he had to face. After flushing the drugs down the toilet, he realised that he was in debt to his drug suppliers for the sum of £10,000. Amazingly, praise God, at the time of speaking to me, that amount had decreased to just £900. However, his relationships were also badly affected by his life choices. He had been awful to his girlfriend and mother of his child for years, and her family hated him. During our conversation, he asked me, "How do I win them over, and how will I keep my girlfriend, as I sense I should not be having sex with her outside of marriage?"

I told him that this is where the Holy Spirit will help him further; that if he continued to walk with God faithfully for the rest of his life, then his girlfriend's family would see the lasting transformation God can bring to a wretched sinner's life. As for his girlfriend, I told him to continue to bring her to church, pray for her salvation, demonstrate godliness as the head of their house and honour God, his girlfriend and his son... by planning to make her his wife.

I wait to hear the next chapter of this story and entrust everyone involved in it to Jesus.

You see, surely, nothing is impossible when we truly surrender our lives to God, as we have a helper in the Holy Spirit! The call may be tough going for the short-term, but the rewards are eternal and *truly brilliant*!

10

A movement too far?

PRESS THE PAUSE BUTTON

When it comes to the LGBTQ+ movement...

> *It seems that the world is no longer just following a policy of tolerance towards this movement; it is proactively marketing a new alternative to God's creative order.*

Is this statement true?

And if it is, is there cause for concern?

Those of you who have been paying close attention will recognise these words from a previous section of my book. I repeat them here to demonstrate how important it is that we ask questions of the nature of the LGBTQ+ movement and its potential impact on the Modern-day Church as well as our communities.

Consider a moment. Just how many references to LGBTQ+ can you see in society around us?

It is not hard to spot them.

In our workplaces, the focus of 'Diversity and Inclusion' policies being used as a platform to champion the LGBTQ+ cause is now required. In many cases these policies are actively encouraged by the introduction of a league table by Stonewall pitting businesses against one another to be perceived as truly embracing LGBTQ+ without any discrimination, ranking them specifically on their degree of diversity and inclusion.[45] Although I caveat that workplaces should be inclusive of all, workplaces must be mindful not to overemphasise one community and it is important to respect individual religious beliefs. In turn, regardless of religious beliefs, every individual should be given respect no matter their race, gender, sexual orientation and more.

In our schools, likewise, we see a huge focus placed on actively teaching LGBTQ+ and neutral gender within the curriculum as well as a move to introduce gender-neutral toilets. Did you know that in London, in March 2022, one particular school was purportedly teaching its pupils that there are, in fact, sixty-four different genders?[46]

I mean, seriously! Is no one even marginally concerned about the confusion this could cause?

Even in our town infrastructure, with the increasing number of road crossings painted in rainbows to represent the Pride symbol of LGBTQ+, we can see the presence of this movement. Hang on, wasn't the rainbow God's creation? Didn't God gift it to Noah and his family following the flood as a sign of His faithfulness; a promise of His unchangeable character that He would never destroy the world by flooding again and could be trusted to keep His Word (Genesis 9)? Why has the rainbow been appropriated by the LGBTQ+ movement? Especially, when, most recently, it was a symbol of the hope provided by doctors, nurses and carers across the British NHS, battling against Covid-19 on our behalf?

All this makes me press the pause button and ask myself, *Whoa, what is really going on here?*

Is there an agenda behind this movement and if so, what is it? Furthermore, how can we as believers respond to this movement in a way that is honouring to God?

At present, all over the world Christians are rightly pointing out the need to lovingly support those individuals who are questioning their sexual orientation. And, let me be noticeably clear: they are absolutely right to offer loving support in every way. There is no cause for Christians anywhere to show disrespect or a lack of compassion towards anyone who decides to live a life that is not in line with the understanding of sexuality in Scripture explained in this book.

That said, whilst there are people, businesses, churches, and Christians passionately looking to champion the LGBTQ+ movement, the fact that the movement appears increasingly pushy in recent times leads me to feel that there is a greater strategy and end goal behind the movement than first meets the eye. It appears to be more than supporting the minority group; I suggest that there seems to be an agenda to convert more people to an LGBTQ+ lifestyle – by which I mean encouraging others to explore their sexual orientation and seek to experiment with orientations other than heterosexual.

A GROWING MOVEMENT

Considering the evidence

In May 2021, Reuters published a report documenting the huge changes in our social landscape:

LONDON (Thomson Reuters Foundation) - More Britons than ever before identify as lesbian, gay or bisexual (LGB), meaning the nation's gay and bi community grew

> *by more than 15% in a year to reach 1.4 million people, the latest government figures showed on Thursday.*
>
> *"People aged 16 to 24 continue to be the most likely to identify as LGB, however the proportion of older adults identifying as LGB, while much smaller, is also increasing," McClure added in a statement.*[47]

I'm not sure we can account for this increase by judging those who have been concealing their sexual orientation for years to be the cause. I think what is more likely is that we can see evidence of an agenda to push LGBTQ+ on young people, particularly in schools, and that this push is having a marked effect on gender identity.

There is however, one more elephant in the room.

We have already spoken of all the initiatives throughout businesses and schools to ensure inclusion of all people. However, something we have not yet addressed in this book is the way people are treated when they do *not* toe the line with this movement which supposedly champions love and inclusion.

In 2021, a landmark moment occurred when Professor Kathleen Stock proved to the world that freedom of speech is only valid if your speech is in line with the leading agenda of the day.[48]

Professor Stock had written a book exploring the idea that gender identity is a 'socially significant' phenomenon rather than being about biological sex. As a result of raising this question however, Stock was branded a transphobic, which she vehemently denied.

In the wake of these accusations, Professor Stock's colleagues turned on her, even inciting students against her further by telling them she was harmful for those identifying as trans people. She was targeted with hate speech on social media, there were pictures of students holding placards with "stock out" on them, and she described seeing her name on posters on the walls all around her workplace.

Similarly, many will remember the Ashers Bakery Ruling in 2014, just seven years earlier, when a bakery owned by Christians refused to ice a cake in support of gay marriage, for reasons of faith. They were sued, lost their case, and then it was later overruled in their favour.[49]

More recently, to highlight the increased control of the LGBTQ+ movement on organisations, an interesting report appeared on the BBC News website on 14 October 2021 entitled 'Stonewall's influence on BBC and Ofcom revealed'. The article reveals the extent of LGBTQ+ charity Stonewall in public bodies, after it overstepped its mark in recent dealings with the BBC and Ofcom.

The report said:

A number of high-profile organisations have left Stonewall's schemes in recent months amid growing controversy about the influence of the group on public policy.[50]

Stonewall was running a programme called 'Diversity Champion' whereby they offered a scheme advising employers on diversity and inclusion for a set fee.

As we can see from these real-life examples, for anyone who opposes the LGBTQ+ movement there is a potential risk of being publicly disgraced, harassed or even sued. In the case of Professor Stock, whilst not headed by Stonewall, the LGBTQ+ campaigning levelled against her had a great impact on her mental health. In the wake of the accusations made against her, she had to give up her job, and likely faces ongoing pain and financial burdens as a result.[51] Yet, the ostracising that Stock experienced was not for any 'hate speech', rather for posing an alternative view on the nature of gender identity.

In the light of this evidence, therefore, is it not reasonable to question whether Stonewall and the LGBTQ+ campaign have become too powerful?

In my opinion, it seems like there is a very controlling spirit behind this movement – one which is prepared to check every area of society and every institutional body for compliance to the movement's rules, otherwise they will make an example of those organisations.

Of course, it is right that there is tolerance throughout society, and it is absolutely right that no one of the LGBTQ+ community should ever feel threatened, isolated, unloved or unwelcomed. But what about when viewed from the other angle? In a nation like the United Kingdom which claims to champion free speech, is it right for speakers to be oppressed publicly, just because they choose to hold a different view?

Providing that view is presented respectfully and humbly, why should it not also be acceptable?

And, if it is not considered acceptable, I would gently suggest that activists must be careful, lest in their efforts to defend the oppressed they become as oppressors themselves.

In my opinion, this collective evidence leads me to believe that the LGBTQ+ movement has become more deliberate in pushing an agenda, seemingly taking no prisoners and exhibiting little compassion towards those who do not comply with its ideologies.

I wonder, how long do the national and international Church have before this matter really lands at *their* doorstep? And how long before individual pastors or church congregations who uphold a biblical conservative perspective of same sex relationships, are labelled homophobes and publicly shunned?

As I remarked previously, there is a loud voice in favour of the Church embracing the LGBTQ+ movement and the changes it will mean for church doctrine, *but there seems to be an intermittent whisper from those who wish to uphold the Word of God correctly.*

Whether we like it or not, this debate is beginning to heat up and persecution for the conservative Church is already on the way according to former evangelical favourite Reverend Steve Chalke who spoke on the issue in 2020 (when 'Q+' had not yet been added to the acronym):

> *When I began to welcome LGBT into my church,
> the Evangelicals threw the charity I founded out
> of their alliance. But I believe what amounts to
> the abuse of LGBT people by churches is likely to
> soon see a crop of high-profile prosecutions.*[52]

Does this mean that anything other than full affirmation of same-sex issues will be met with protests, or even lawsuits as Steve Chalke implies here? Might persecution be around the corner in the form of the British government refusing financial support in granting Gift Aid to churches who have a legal charity status?

It's certainly a possibility.

More than meets the eye

To understand why this movement is as strident as it is, I believe we need to return to the biblical record and consider things from God's perspective.

As Ephesians 6 highlights, it is vital that all of us recognise there is a deeper level of struggle going on in our world, one that is taking place in the heavenly realms:

> *For our struggle is not against flesh and blood, but against the rulers, against the authorities, against the powers of this dark world and against the spiritual forces of evil in the heavenly realms.*

(Ephesians 6:12, NIV)

True, it is important not to look for the devil over our shoulder at every turn. However, it is equally important to probe the agendas of our culture and determine whether they are God-honouring. And this is key when we come to the same-sex debate and understanding what God's Word says so that we may view sexuality and holiness through His eyes not our own.

Could it be that Satan is driving the aggression behind the LGBTQ+ movement which, ultimately, is bringing mass confusion on our society, increasing gender identity crises and creating persecution against those who do not toe the line or swallow what culture is dictating?

It's worth asking the question, even if it may appear rather extreme.

The Bible says that Satan is a master of disguise and masquerades as an angel of light (2 Corinthians 11:14). The Bible also tells us that he is called the prince of this world and it is not hard to see the demonic influence at work in our modern-day society (John 14:30, 2 Corinthians 4:4).

Neither is it hard to discern the work of Satan in history. In fact, I believe if we look closely enough at the events in the world, we will see Satan's characteristics showing up repeatedly.

For instance, when he tempts Jesus in the wilderness, he tries to persuade Him to be self-sufficient in turning the stones into bread; he tries to persuade Jesus to elevate Himself offering Him all the kingdoms of the world; he tries to persuade Jesus to worship him. He does this using twisted scriptures and temptations - it's very much a parallel of Satan's temptation of Adam and Eve in the Garden of Eden (compare the accounts of Jesus' temptation in Matthew 4:1-11 with Adam and Eve's temptation in Genesis 3).

This model of Satan's temptation has continued throughout time. Today, his chief agenda remains persuading people to believe that they don't need God, to convince them that they are self-sufficient. He attempts to realise this agenda by generating addictions to all sorts of worldly things such as wealth, achievement, alcohol, and more. He causes believers to question Scripture and say, "Surely, God *didn't* say that? Surely, a loving God *won't* let people die? Surely, in these days with such a loving God, the Scriptures about sexuality *don't* really mean same-sex relationships are unacceptable to God? Surely not?"

Always, the devil comes back to the same tack: questioning whether what God has said is the last authority on the matter, questioning His God-breathed Word.

However, although Satan's ultimate agenda is to steal, kill and destroy (John 10:10), he can sometimes overplay his hand - something I have seen demonstrated in my own experiences when I have encountered demonic activity.

Let me give you an example...

On one occasion, I was asked to pray for a young woman whose aunty was convinced there was demonic activity going on due to her niece's erratic behaviour manifested by a particularly unpleasant outburst. Usually, the woman was known to be very sweet, but her outburst was so severe that the police were called and found themselves faced with a very vicious young woman, completely out of character. The woman was aggressive, threatening, and uncooperative... the police didn't know what to do with her.

The morning following the outbursts, I was called to visit and speak with the young woman and to assess her. From the minute I arrived, I could sense she was not quite right. I was certain there was some sort of spiritual hold on her, but she seemed to be playing a very sweet and quiet game with me. We chatted for some time, and she answered my questions and was polite throughout, but I could see she was holding something back.

In the end I said, "Now, I'm going to pray for you, then I'm going to leave. But before I do that, I'm going to read Scripture to you." With that, I pulled out my Bible... Suddenly, the young woman started to squint her eyes at me, her face started to change, and she began to hiss at me.

At that point, I cannot remember if I said it or thought it, but I believe I may have said something along the lines of, "OK, *there* you are."

The young woman did have a demonic influence in her life, and afterwards I learned that her father had been involved in the occult, something that always gives the devil an entry point into unsuspecting lives.

It is never pleasant to encounter demonic activity and any incident where prayer for deliverance is required must be approached with great caution and discernment. However, I share this story to emphasise that Satan and his demonic army like to hide. As I mentioned earlier, what I have also noticed is that in the act of hiding, they often overplay their hand, particularly when standing in the presence of the people of God carrying the Holy Spirit of God!

In the case of LGBTQ+, could it be that the movement is a cloak for satanic activity; that behind a so-called harmless desire to promote love and inclusion for all people, there is, in fact, something more sinister at work? Again, this is not to treat the LGBTQ+ community of individuals with any disrespect; as God's people, we must always love others, however, we need to ask ourselves whether the movement itself is going too far by re-drawing what society looks like? Will it eventually lead to increased anxiety and mental health issues? Will it damage the health of family units in the future?

Have we failed as believers to discern this? Have we been blinded by 'the prince of this age' (2 Corinthians 4:4, John 14:30)? Or have we even adopted an extra-biblical and warped perspective of who God really is?

You see, the gospel Jesus instructed us to share in the Great Commission is not a fluffy fairy-tale. God is all loving, yes, but the Bible also says some things that may shock us, things that seem to run counter to the image of a God of love. Just look at Isaiah 53:10:

> **Yet it was the LORD's will to crush him** and cause him to suffer **(King James Version reads: ['it pleased God to bruise Him'])**,
> and though the LORD makes his life an offering for sin,
> he will see his offspring and prolong his days,
> and the will of the LORD will prosper in his hand.
>
> (My emphasis added, NIV and KJV)

It may jar with the reader to see that it pleased God to crush His own Son on the cross. However, I do not believe the emphasis of this passage is the pleasure of crushing His Son; rather it refers to the pleasure God felt knowing that His Son would lay down His life to save the world (John 15:13). God's plan was to rid the world of sin, to save multitudes for eternity and set them free from the ownership of evil and death. Therefore, the sacrifice of one man for the salvation of many was ethically pleasing to God - although it would be painful for Him, because the man who would suffer was His own Son whom He publicly affirmed: 'This is my Son, whom I love; with him I am well pleased' (Matthew 3:16-17, NIV).

When Jesus hung on the cross, Satan must have thought he was victorious. Imagine how hard it must have been for Satan to realise that through his greatest masterful plan to wreak havoc and destruction, he had actually carried out God's will, to God's exact timing!

Even when evil thinks it has won the day, isn't it fantastic that it is only serving up its own defeat in the will and plan of God!

A NOTE OF CHALLENGE...

So, then, if we conclude that the spirit behind the LGBTQ+ movement is counter to God's blueprint for His world, we can begin to think more clearly.

We can make distinctions between those who may identify with the movement and what the movement is driving at.

We can love the former as Jesus does and we can treat with caution the latter, *but* we can also choose to be bold and question the agenda that is infiltrating our societies.

Stop for a moment and imagine the media reports that would appear today if Jesus was walking the earth and spoke up against divorce as He did during His years of ministry...

There would be complete outrage!

Or what about when Jesus spoke of gouging out a person's eye or cutting off a hand that causes them to sin?

In today's world, people would be up in arms!

Of course, He may have been speaking figuratively, but I'm sure that Jesus and His' controversial teachings would be considered majorly offensive to the societal 'norms' of our world today.

So then, how should we respond to this movement if we want to uphold love and honour God by our actions and attitudes?

It's helpful to consider the example of Jesus further.

How did Jesus react when faced with the need to love wholeheartedly whilst also standing up for truth with regard to sin?

Well, when Jesus was called to stone the adulterous woman in John 8, He compassionately and vocally defended her with great wisdom. After those wanting to stone her had all left, He had this moving conversation with her:

Jesus straightened up and asked her, "Woman, where are they? Has no one condemned you?"

"No one, sir," she said.

"Then neither do I condemn you," Jesus declared. "Go now and leave your life of sin."

(John 8:10-11, NIV)

Jesus defended the woman and showed her compassion and dignity. He then went on to do something that demonstrates to all believers today the essential ingredient to being true gospel evangelists… He told her to leave her life of sin.

He did not avoid the key issue but squarely confronted it and invited the woman to do the same. So, He defended her, corrected and rebuked the oppressors, showed her compassion and dignity, and then pointed her to a new life without sin.

He never overlooked her sin.

Following the example of Jesus, we must choose to defend our fellow believers in the LGBTQ+ community; we must love them, show compassion when they encounter struggles, and crucially, we must be honest with them about what it means for them to pursue the kingdom-life as revealed by God's Word.

Then, we must extend extra love and compassion as we journey with them in that decision and whatever sacrifices and challenges it may mean for them.

As for the LGBTQ+ movement which I have already stated is distinct from individuals who comprise the LGBTQ+ community: ultimately, it is time to switch on our spiritual antennae and be alert to the changing times around us.

My message to the Church of believers today is simple: we are called to bring one kingdom to bear on the earth, and it is *God's Kingdom.*

The time where the culture around us dictates who we are and how we live must end! I believe it is time to stand up and say "enough is enough" when it comes to what our children are being taught, what is being imposed on businesses and what is being painted on our roads. It is time for God's prophets of the day to stand up and speak up as John the Baptist did.

We don't need to be unkind.

We don't need to be unwelcoming.

But we do need to be *uncompromising!*

Let's close with words from a parable Jesus recounts to His followers, about a judge who does not care about God. They are sobering for us all:

> *However, when the Son of Man comes,*
> *will he find faith on the earth?'*

(Matthew 18:8, NIV)

When Jesus returns, what will he find in *us*? A people who acts justly according to His Word, or a people who values the world's friendship over God's truth?

Loving all people is a command of God but doing it whilst upholding God's instruction was the model Jesus demonstrated.

We can love people without agreeing with or affirming their lifestyle; we can disagree without drawing blood or being harsh.

When Jesus returns, will He find a good and faithful servant in His Church?

Where are the prophets of the day?

Pastors, what are you doing with your call? Are you willing to collaborate with Him in clarifying the biblical record without compromise and committing to seeing sexuality and holiness through His eyes?

Even at the potential risk of being persecuted and called a homophobe?

Churches, the world and chastisement

AN UNEXPECTED WORD FROM THE LORD

It was a normal Sunday morning at the beginning of December 2019.

I wasn't preaching. I wasn't even conducting the service. Instead, I was given the rare chance to simply sit in the congregation and be part of it without leading anything...

Or so I thought.

The praise time was great, and the sermon was good, too. Next thing I knew, the service was ending, and I suddenly became very uncomfortable, as though I needed to get up and say something that would seem very odd. I didn't hear a voice; I just had an overwhelming sense I needed to get out of my seat and tell the whole congregation a message that would make me look like I had completely lost the plot.

After grappling with the idea that I might not be popular after I delivered the message, and that people would probably think I was nuts, I decided to get up and speak. I took the microphone from the service leader, and I told the congregation I sensed a need to share an important message. This is what it was...

"There is a storm coming. A time is coming when we won't be able to meet as a church in the way we currently do. Something is going to happen over the next five or so years that is going to radically change church as we know it. During this time, even the Church will turn on itself..."

I sat down feeling perplexed and a little embarrassed. I wondered what people must have thought of their once-sane pastor.

Following the word I shared, Diana, one of our leaders, walked forward and took the mic herself. She said: "I believe Mike has just had a word from the Lord. We must pray and take it seriously."

It all seemed rather weird at the time, but later that month the Wuhan situation, which we now know was the beginning of the Covid-19 pandemic, started to kick off. I never imagined it would affect any other town or city, let alone the whole world. I had never heard of a pandemic before. I didn't listen attentively at school so I never could have put two and two together.

We all know the story from there. Within months, Covid-19 had erupted in our own country, the United Kingdom, to such a degree that lockdowns followed, bringing with them the necessity of closing churches nationwide. In the case of Reigate Baptist, although I initially told the church family we would not formally close because we live by faith and not by sight, our church did close for a time – along with many other churches worldwide. Why? Because I wished us to be above reproach in honouring our government which is something God Himself has instructed us to do (1 Peter 2:13).

I am sad we never recorded the word that I shared, but at the time it occurred, we had a practice of recording only the sermons themselves. That said, there were at least 250-300 people present to witness what I said that day. God works in mysterious ways...

I'll be honest with you; I look at most people and consider them much more 'spiritual' than me. This is no ego trip or attempt to get people to say, "Wow, isn't he prophetic!" (I'm really not!) But, on a few occasions, I have said something, and, to my surprise, it has come to pass. I believe this is partly why I never panicked as a pastor in times of lockdown; I was comfortable making decisions with the eldership team and I was happy to get it wrong at times – I am certain that I did.

"Why is this even relevant?" I hear you ask. And why does 'chastisement' feature in the title of this chapter, seemingly, a very heavy subject? How does this fit in with a desire to explain what God's perspective of sexuality and holiness is and how we as believers can keep love and truth in tandem in communicating that to the world?

Well, it is relevant for two reasons.

Firstly, because I found myself surprised and rather shocked by some of the famous Christian voices heard during the pandemic. They exhibited a range of very diverse perspectives which I didn't feel were entirely biblical.

Whilst some said words to this effect: 'the Coronavirus doesn't have the smell of God about it', others produced lengthy video episodes stating that 'God doesn't send anything bad upon people... so we cannot possibly attribute the virus to Him.' As I watched and listened, I sat there thinking... *Whilst God may not have sent the virus, He could have prevented it at any time He chose.* It's important to remember that there are consequences to our actions as humankind: both as a result of the Fall of man in Genesis 3, and the world's rejection of God today. Remember, we reap what we sow (Genesis 6:8).

That said, I understand God to be loving and kind and a God who wants all individuals everywhere to be saved – all of which is attested clearly by the Bible, His Word (Isaiah 54:8, 2 Peter 3:9). However, I cannot simultaneously ignore the other aspects of His character that are manifested through the biblical record in both the Old *and* the New Testament. The grace that has been granted to us through Jesus' death and resurrection does not mean that God's character has changed. His holiness and His justice mean He will not be mocked (Genesis 6:8).

Take for example, the plagues God sent upon the Egyptians in Exodus in the Old Testament and then consider the punishment of death that He dealt upon Ananias and Sapphira in the New Testament book of Acts when they were caught stealing from God (Exodus 7-11, Acts 5:1-11). Is this a God who refuses to send calamity, who doesn't 'send anything bad' upon people?

Well, the plain biblical truth is that God has done it reluctantly in the past, but I think it is equally true that today, God wishes His people to grasp the true significance of repentance, that they might be set apart for Him. As a wise mentor of mine recently remarked to me, could it be that "God is doing something different beyond Calvary (since the death of Jesus for the sins of the world)?"

Of course, we need to keep in mind a faithful representation of who God is in this regard. On the one hand, it would be wrong to depict Him as one who would not punish a rebellious world or His own people, when He feels it is required. On the other, it would be equally wrong if we were to become so extreme in our representations of Him that we emphasise a God who is angry and aggressive, levelling judgment at the world, akin to the lightning bolts and churlish whims of the Greek gods. Our God is not at all like that!

It is true that God has poured out judgment, even on His own people in the past, and there is judgment yet to come: The Bible speaks of the outpouring of God's wrath through the horsemen of the Apocalypse in the last days (Revelation 6). Yet, let us not forget two key things: God sent His Son to pay the price for all sin and His Son Jesus was willing to pay that price. Therefore, *God's dominant characteristic is grace*, and His overwhelming desire for all of us is repentance which leads to forgiveness, salvation and eternity with Him!

We must also remember that God always leaves the door open to repentance that leads to healing – and this too is the narrative that echoes throughout the Bible. There is *always* an opportunity for man to repent and to receive His blessing. It would do us well to remember that the reason we are still alive in this sinful world is because He is showing us patience, declaring:

> *If my people, who are called by my name, will humble themselves and pray and seek my face and turn from their wicked ways, then I will hear from heaven, and I will forgive their sin and will heal their land.*

(2 Chronicles 7:14, NIV)

The second reason my story of that odd word pre-Covid-19 is relevant, is because it has bearing on our subject of how as the Church, we choose to respond to the LGBTQ+ movement and community today.

It is noticeable that no one is speaking publicly about what might happen if churches *do* embrace the LGBTQ+ movement and go all out for redefining what relationships are affirmed by God. Would this not signal a move to a permissive approach to Christianity – where we can decide for ourselves what is sin and what is not?

All this makes me pause and ask myself... *If God is not pleased with churches for embracing what His Word warns us against, will He just overlook it? Will God ignore the fact that His people on earth have deviated from what He has set out in His Word, the Bible, rejecting His will in exchange for the will of the world?*

And I have further questions.

Is it coincidental that the Church in the United Kingdom is declining across many denominations at a time in which we are embracing or considering embracing a redefinition of marriage which is unbiblical? Or could the decline be a sign that God is actively removing His blessing from these churches; the removal of His Holy Spirit who draws new believers?

What's more, could the increase in world conflict, pandemics, financial meltdowns and natural disasters have anything to do with the widespread rejection of God's instruction in the world?

We are not under the Law; we are under grace. However, a world apart from Jesus is not under grace; they are apart from the protection of a loving heavenly Father, and under Satan, the 'ruler of the air,' who desires to steal, kill and destroy (Ephesians 2:2, John 10:10, NIV).

Whether God sends the above-mentioned events, allows them, or simply doesn't intervene, churches need to point the world to the fact that these struggles only exist on the earth because God and His kingdom have been rejected... But, vitally, to do this whilst also proclaiming the *good news*; that we can turn back to God through what Jesus accomplished on the cross and live in anticipation of a restored world when He returns in the End Times.

Now, let's look briefly at the Church before considering the subject of chastisement, further.

Could it be that God is chastising or disciplining His people on account of their having embraced sinfulness and becoming more like the culture around them – in particular, where the topic of this book is concerned when affirming LGBTQ+ relationships? Let's consider how Isaiah 5:20 (NIV) puts it:

> *Woe to those who call evil good*
> *and good evil,*
> *who put darkness for light*
> *and light for darkness,*
> *who put bitter for sweet*
> *and sweet for bitter...*

'Woe' in the Bible is an extremely strong word, and so we must at least ponder the idea that God could and would choose to chastise and discipline His people.

CHASTISEMENT AND THE WORLD

God is loving. Let's not forget this nor overlook the evidence. Even when He sent armies against His own people in the Old Testament, He did not leave them without the hope of liberation and redemption, something seen clearly in 2 Chronicles 7:14 and Jeremiah 36:3 as the voice of God speaks to His people:

> *When **I shut up the heavens so that there is no rain, or command locusts to devour the land or send a plague among my people**, if my people, who are called by my name, will humble themselves and pray and seek my face and turn*

from their wicked ways, then I will hear from heaven, and I will forgive their sin and will heal their land. Now my eyes will be open and my ears attentive to the prayers offered in this place.

(2 Chronicles 7:13-14, NIV, my emphasis added)

*Perhaps when the people of Judah hear about **every disaster, I plan to inflict on them**, they will each turn from their wicked ways; then I will forgive their wickedness and their sin.*

(Jeremiah 36:3, NIV, my emphasis added)

God also gave timings for the duration of punishment, which were revealed to Daniel and Jeremiah who shared God's message with the people. They declared that captivity would end, and God would liberate His people from bondage, giving them an opportunity to return to Him (Daniel 9).

Furthermore, in pointing mankind to His timings and His purpose, we can see God's mercy as part of the equation right from the very beginning of the world when, as a result of the Fall, God compelled Adam and Eve to leave the garden of Eden. To them both as well as to the serpent, God prophesied what we now call 'the evangelion', which is the very first sight we are afforded of the gospel in the Bible. He reveals it in His choice of words to Satan:

*And I will put enmity
between you and the woman,
and between your offspring and hers;
he will crush your head,
and you will strike his heel.*

(Genesis 3:15, NIV)

In other words, God was saying, "I'm sending a saviour to save My people! Satan, you will strike His heel. You will wound

Him," (referring to the cross) "but He will crush your skull" (referring to victory on the cross).

Clearly, we can see that even though God is the God of justice and must pour out the consequences of sin in correct judgment, yet He is gracious and kind to give His people (that includes us) warning, and sometimes even timings for the duration of events and the remedies to our sin.[53]

Whatever His timetable and commitment to love, this does not mean God will not chastise His people or punish a world who has rejected Him.[54] The Bible tells us that God is also a God who is committed to loving discipline just as a loving parent by necessity chooses to discipline their own child:

> *And have you completely forgotten this word*
> *of encouragement that addresses you as a*
> *father addresses his son? It says,*
>
> *"My son, do not make light of the Lord's discipline,*
> *and do not lose heart when he rebukes you, because the Lord*
> *disciplines the one he loves,*
> *and he chastens everyone he accepts as his son."*
>
> *Endure hardship as discipline; God is treating you as his*
> *children. For what children are not disciplined by their father?*

(Hebrews 12:5-7, NIV)

We have already spoken about the world in this book, the way it has promoted awful practices such as abortion, relationships which offend God, racism, the way at times it has neglected to take care of countless foreigners and refugees, produced dishonest politics, idolised money... and many other things outside of God's covenant. In condoning these practices, the world remains under judgment, and what we see happening in the world is proof of that: The world is groaning under the strain of greed and instant gratification and the world suffers the consequences spoken of in Scripture (Romans 6:23, Romans 8:22).

Many people remark to me, "But surely, this is not the case since Jesus has brought in a new covenant of grace..." And my response is to suggest that we ask another question: "Has the world entered that covenant by repentance?" I would argue that in most cases, sadly, the answer is no. Therefore, if the world and individuals are not under that covenant, they reap what they sow. In fact, the Bible states that the world is blinded and directed by Satan, 'the god of this age,' and is in rebellion to God – expressed most starkly in 2 Corinthians 4:4 (NIV):

The god of this age has blinded the minds of unbelievers,
so that they cannot see the light of the gospel that
displays the glory of Christ, who is the image of God.

My inner reasoning runs something like this...

Surely, you can't blame a God, you claim you don't believe in.

You can't expect help from a God you are rejecting and pushing away.

Can you?

I remember watching an interview once, with author and actor, Stephen Fry, during which he was asked what he would say to God if he was faced with Him at the Pearly Gates. His response was interesting:

"Bone cancer in children? What's that all about? How dare you! How dare you create a world where there is such misery that is not our fault! It's not right! It's not right! It's utterly, utterly evil. Why should I respect a capricious, mean-minded God who

creates a world which is so full of injustice and pain... that's what I would say."

The interviewer responded, *"And you think you are going to get in?"*

To which Fry rejoindered: *"No... and I wouldn't want to, I wouldn't want to get in on his terms – they're wrong. However, if I died and it was Plato, Hades, and the twelve Greek gods, then I'd have more truck with it because the Greeks didn't pretend not to be more human in their appetites and in their capriciousness and their unreasonableness... they didn't pretend to be all seeing and all wise, all kind, all beneficent, because the God who created this universe is quite clearly a maniac."*[55]

Fry then went on to talk about a species of insect whose whole life cycle is to burrow into the eyes of children and blind them, implying therefore that He sees God as mean and asking why anyone would follow Him. But is this view not flawed?

In stating the existence of this insect, is Fry not effectively attributing its existence to God as a creator – the God that he claims does not exist?

How can we square that?

It is true that the view Fry expresses here, is one that is commonly held by many individuals in the world; that, if there is a God, then He is utterly evil for the mess He has made in the world. But here's the thing, did any insect burrow into eyes *before* the fall of mankind? Did cancer exist *before* the devil persuaded Eve to exalt herself and Adam to God's level of knowledge and power? The answer is an emphatic no!

In fact, I would suggest that the entire world is falling apart because humans fell first! Humans are destroying the world and blaming God for it, and that is why judgment still stands and why Stephen Fry cannot blame God for the world as it is - because the world the way God intends it to be, (heaven), is yet to come.

My prayer is that Stephen Fry will encounter the Lord soon, as I really want him to be in God's precious kingdom one day! Yet, the reality is, unless people humble themselves and accept their part in the evil world that they blame God for, they will not enter heaven, as their eyes will remain blinded to the truth that they *need* a Saviour. Put very simply, there is nothing bad in heaven; God cannot and will not permit it entry into His Holy presence.

So, although the world is disappointed in the world that exists, the irony is that individuals in the world cannot blame a God they do not profess to believe. In His stead they can only blame themselves and rue their evil decisions...

The world is rather like a man who buys a car, drives it too hard, breaks it and then demands his money back – all the time abdicating responsibility and deluding himself that he is actually culpable for the outcome.

Ultimately, the world's only hope is a saviour on a cross who died to pay the price for people's wrongdoing; that by true repentance, every individual in the world might live in relationship with God for ever. The great news is, *that Saviour is available in Jesus Christ*! He is only a prayer away and He is waiting and willing to respond to every heart of every individual who sincerely repents! It is this saviour Jesus, who will fix the world anew and believe me, there will be no disappointment with the world that is to come!

CHASTISEMENT AND THE CHURCH

"But what about God's people?" I hear you say. "What has chastisement got to do with the Church, and do we merit it?

As I mentioned earlier, God disciplines those He loves as a father disciplines his children.[56]

Let's face it: The Church is a very mixed bag right now.

I've come across churches who embrace and promote LGBTQ+; I know of churches who allow other faith groups to pray to their god in the church building or permit yoga to take place on their premises; others have relegated the preaching of God's Word and placed more emphasis on the peripheral issues; and some have opted to support abortion.

Sadly, many churches have an uneven balance of Word and Spirit. Many are heavy on the Word but closed to the Holy Spirit. Others are so Spirit-focused, God's Word gets barely a mention.

It seems like some churches have become more like a weekly concert than a weekly service; their leaders lack spiritual depth and are more concerned by fame and international acclaim than giving Jesus central place as Lord and saviour in the hearts of those they disciple.

Seriously, let's stop and ask ourselves the question:

If God was to write the letters to the churches, as He did in the opening chapters of Revelation, what would He say to us today?

We need only look at the News to see how God's Modern-day Church is being represented...

It is certainly sobering!

In recent years the News has featured stories of many negative portrayals of Christianity: Churches who have been accused of concealing child sex abuse incidents over many years; major mega churches exposed for moral failures; and some of the most effective Christian thinkers of our time having passed away, likewise with a whole Pandora's box of sexual accusations...

What on earth are we playing at!

Where is God's Church, called to be holy because He is holy? (Leviticus 11:44, 1 Peter 1:16)

Are we not meant to be the light of the world?

Or have I misread my Bible?

It's time for the Church to wake up!

It's time for us to take our morality seriously!

It's time for us to realise that God sees everything we do and everything we think!

It's time to ask ourselves the tougher questions, like...

Are we, as believers, leading the lost deeper into the wilderness, further away from God, by our behaviour?

I know that, to some, this may sound completely outrageous, and I am not mincing my words. But I believe it is time to take down the masks we are all culpable for wearing on occasion and throw away the pretence.

Let's admit it: We *all* have issues.

Many of us are broken by particular things in particular ways for particular reasons.

So, let's stop making excuses! Let's get on our knees and pray for forgiveness. Then, let's stand up, committed afresh to doing things God's way, hold each other accountable and show the world what the people of God *really* look like!

Finally, are there consequences for the Church if its witness is doing more harm than good? Confusing the lost by living sinful lives, and worse, embracing sinful practices clearly prohibited in the Bible? Certainly, I believe there are consequences...

Could it be that God allowed the Church to shut its doors because it wasn't covering itself in glory being open?

Could it be that the self-focused concerts, the promiscuous leaders, the lack of reverent fear for the Lord and all the other things I've mentioned already have caused the Lord to shake the Church and give us the opportunity to repent and rethink how we do and are 'church'?

Could it be that the reason the British Government found it so easy to decide to close churches at one point during the Covid-19 pandemic is because we are so liberally linked to state that they knew we were in their pocket?

Could it be that we hold no obvious power and authority in the eyes of the world that the Government could see no use for the Church? Even though in World War II, it was the National Day of Prayer when King George VI publicly called the nation to their knees that brought about the miracle of Dunkirk.

I know this message isn't going to be popular!

The truth is, I am hungry for God and always have been. But I'm not in the least hungry to be part of a self-serving, God-denying, 'tea on the lawn', Holy Spirit-ignoring Church anymore. (Incidentally, I do like tea and lawns, but hopefully, you get the picture. If it's just a question of having a 'nice picnic', then it's putting on a show of keeping up appearances and showing off the best china, rather than connecting with God spiritually and being transformed.)

I know which one I'd opt for!

I can fill a church of people on Sundays wanting to sing their favourite songs. I can even fill a church happy to put up with my sermons... but can I get more than twenty people to a prayer meeting?

Usually, no.

My old boss at Barclays Bank used to say, "Looks like they are giving out redundancies again Mike, last one out turns the lights out." If we are going to be of no use in these perilous days, perhaps the greatest wisdom we could apply would be to do what the Government did for us in the period of the Pandemic: to turn the lights out on the Church.

Don't get me wrong, I'm not calling for the Church to die out and extinguish itself altogether. Plus, I know the Church did some wonderful things during the periods of lockdown - and perhaps this was where we saw the true heart of true believers at work. Or perhaps Covid-19 was the wake-up call that led to action. The bottom line is, we cannot ignore the fact that before the Pandemic hit, the Church was in a questionable state for the reasons I've already mentioned; a mixed bag that appeared to have lost its compass and supplanted Christ for culture. Neither can we ignore the fact that today, many churches are affirming things like the LGBTQ+ movement. They did it before Covid and now, in its wake, they are continuing to promote the agenda of culture, even though as evidenced in our chapters exploring the Bible, it is clearly *not* biblically affirmed by God.

In some cases, churches in the United Kingdom closed for over a year!

Now, let's take a step back… and consider asking God why He *did* allow it.

We may unearth a story like that of Joshua 7 where there was sin hidden in the camp of the Israelites and God refused to go up and fight for His people. And what was the outcome? Thirty-six of them died. Then, bereaved, and chastened, Joshua lay prostrate beside the Ark of the Covenant, and sought God for the answer to events. He soon received it and God's words were uncompromising:

> The LORD said to Joshua, "Stand up! What are you doing down on your face? Israel has sinned; they have violated my covenant, which I commanded them to keep. They have taken some of the devoted things; they have stolen, they have lied, they have put them with their own possessions. That is why the Israelites cannot stand against their enemies; they turn their backs and run because they have been made liable to destruction. I will not be with you anymore unless you destroy whatever among you is devoted to destruction."
>
> (Joshua 7:10-12, NIV)

In other words, rid yourselves of sin!

I wonder, would God speak such words to us, His people today?

Could it be that in our efforts to be liked, in our commitment to show the kind of unrelenting, utterly forgiving love that Jesus did, we have forgotten something important; that truly loving someone also requires truth, boundaries, and even discipline.

*So, have we become too nice yet, in reality, unloving in **not** addressing the things that are a danger to those we profess to love?*

In the case of the LGBTQ+ community, welcoming all people regardless of their sexuality, loving them as we would anyone else, but **not** stating that God does not affirm homosexual practice.

In our churches, is it not time *now*, to speak the truth in love, hold each other accountable, and maintain biblical church discipline – all in tandem?

I cannot overemphasise however, that it must be done in a *non-judgmental*, loving manner, always. For, we must remember that it is the Holy Spirit who convicts and the Holy Spirit who transforms – not us! And equally, we must remember that we are all sinful and all need that transformation!

Chastisement and discipline feature throughout the Bible, and are recurring themes for God's people, the Israelites, who were continuously chastised for disobeying God's instruction, as evidenced by several examples below:

Consider Numbers 14:21-23 (NIV):

Nevertheless, as surely as I live and as surely as the glory of the LORD fills the whole earth, not one of those who saw my glory and the signs I performed in Egypt and in the wilderness but who disobeyed me and tested me ten times—not one of them will ever see the land I promised on oath to their ancestors. No one who has treated me with contempt will ever see it.

Or, how about 2 Kings 18:11-12 (NIV) that describes the deportation of the Israelites to Assyria:

The king of Assyria deported Israel to Assyria and settled them in Halah, in Gozan on the Habor River and in towns of the Medes. This happened because they had not obeyed the LORD their God but had violated his covenant—all that Moses the servant of the

Lᴏʀᴅ commanded. *They neither listened to the commands nor carried them out.*

Likewise, King David was chastised after having an affair and instigating murder (2 Samuel 12), and the disciple Peter was chastised by Jesus several times. (It would be hard to argue that Jesus words in Matthew 16:23, 'Get behind me Satan!' could be anything other than chastisement.) Yet, God chastises His people in the hope that they will return to their heavenly Father who loves them and wants the best for them, *always!*

A NOTE OF ENCOURAGEMENT...

HANG ON A MINUTE! After all that chat on chastisement and discipline, let me take a moment to cool down... I want to return to the wise words of my mentor, which I mentioned earlier in this chapter: "Mike, I think God is doing something different beyond Calvary..."

I believe he is right; God is much more gracious than I have so far explained. My mentor went on to tell me about the olive trees we saw together during a recent trip to Israel, growing on the Mount of Olives. He described how, when cut down to a stump, new life grows through the stump of the trees and bares new olive leaves. He said, "Mike, I believe this same thing is happening to churches all the time."

Let me say it again: God is gracious.

I don't believe it is certain we will see scenes like those of Exodus 8-10 and the Plagues that devastated Egypt. I don't expect to see locusts filling churches today, or plagues killing off swathes of Christians. However, if churches continue to embrace what is unbiblical, I believe they will dwindle as the blessing of the Lord leaves – and become as a stump.

Furthermore, if they do remain unrepentant, I believe they will disappear to be replaced by new life – just like the olive trees on the Mount of Olives.

Jesus clearly warned the church of Ephesus of exactly this in Revelations 2:4-5 (NIV):

> *Yet I hold this against you: You have forsaken the love you had at first. Consider how far you have fallen! Repent and do the things you did at first. If you do not repent, **I will come to you and remove your lampstand from its place**.*

(my emphasis added)

We need a renewal in the Church today, and it starts with this:

God's people taking God seriously and getting on their knees in prayer and repentance.

It means a rediscovery of fasting and prayer and real sacrificial service for the Lord.

It means at times we will have to speak up on big issues of the day that are leading the world and the Church further away from God.

The question is, "Who's with me?"

In the words of Evan Roberts, the Welsh revivalist, 'Bend us, Lord!'

My cry to everyone including myself is:

Do something, we need you!

Wake up Christians!

12

Sharing Jesus with the LGBTQ+ community

A CONUNDRUM FOR BELIEVERS

One of the most painful questions I have been asking myself throughout my prayerful reflection on the whole LGBTQ+ debate is:

How will we reach this community of people if we say anything outside of the Genesis blueprint for sexuality is a sin?

It really has caused me great distress.

I cannot go the same way that many Christians around me have chosen to in disregarding Scripture.

I cannot find a way around Scripture by ignoring its true context, writing off the Law of God on our hearts which is revealed in the Holiness Code, and simply saying "Jesus is love" therefore it's all fine now as we're "living under grace".

At the same time, I genuinely have a love for all people and whatever their sexuality preferences, it doesn't bother me personally. What bothers me about any individual is this: I want them to know God, I want to be a friend to them, and I want to be in the eternal kingdom with them.

So, what can we do if we do not see the affirmation of the LGBTQ+ lifestyle in Scripture, yet desperately want to lead individuals to the kingdom-life that Jesus offers?

I need to be very clear, here, and clarify that this is not a question of imposing what is termed as conversion therapy upon an individual who may say that they are struggling with the question of their sexuality. Personally, I do not agree at all with conversion therapy as it has been interpreted in the past through the usage of barbaric treatments like electric shock and some forms of 'deliverance'. However, I do wish to state that, in my opinion, the current conversion therapy bill under consideration in the United Kingdom merits closer inspection of its scope when and if it should become law. This is because I feel it has the capacity to infringe on freedom of speech with its scope to penalise, and perhaps even prosecute churches and charities whose vision may be simply to come alongside an individual who has requested pastoral support on this matter. Furthermore, it does concern me that the bill also has the capacity to silence the Church in explaining what the Bible has to say on this subject.

Let me reiterate our main question here:

So, what can we do if we do not see the affirmation of the LGBTQ+ lifestyle in Scripture, yet desperately want to lead individuals to the kingdom-life that Jesus offers?

Jesus was presented with a similar question when He met the rich young ruler in Luke 18. The rich man asked Jesus how he could inherit eternal life. Jesus replied telling him to obey the Ten Commandments, to which the man responded saying he had obeyed the Law from his childhood.

What Jesus said next is almost identical to the challenge that confronted the man who so desperately wanted the precious pearl when he chose to sell everything for the kingdom of God. Jesus' words to the rich man were these:

> *You still lack one thing. Sell everything you have and give to the poor, and you will have treasure in heaven. Then come, follow me.*

(Luke 18:22, NIV)

In this conversation, Jesus again points out the value of the kingdom of God. He highlights the fact that it requires us to put to death our will, our desires, our sinful character, our old way of life... everything that stands in the way of us fully embracing God and His way of life for us!

Faced with such a challenge, how did the man respond?

> *When he heard this, he became very sad, because he was very wealthy. Jesus looked at him and said, "How hard it is for the rich to enter the kingdom of God! Indeed, it is easier for a camel to go through the eye of a needle than for someone who is rich to enter the kingdom of God."*

(Luke 18:23-25, NIV)

This is the sad reality of choosing idols over God.

We need to ask ourselves: *What are we choosing to make more important than following Jesus?*

This includes anything that we cannot give up for Jesus.

This includes our sexuality...

Should this dishearten us?

I mean, if we have a view of sexuality that we believe is biblical, but the world and many churches around us refuse to agree with our position, does this mean the task ahead of us is impossible?

Not according to Jesus.

Having challenged the young ruler to sell all his wealth for the kingdom, He goes on to challenge the listening crowd with an incredible statement:

> *Those who heard this asked, "Who then can be saved?"*
> *Jesus replied,* **"What is impossible with**
> **man is possible with God."**

(Luke 18:26-27 NIV, my emphasis added)

Nothing is impossible for God!

That's right, *nothing* is impossible for Him.

Let's consider His track record.

When a legalistic Saul breathed out murderous threats against the Church, when he was bent on eradicating the people of God, Jesus appeared to him and said, 'Why do you persecute me?' (Acts 9:4, NIV).

We all know what happened next: Saul underwent a complete transformation. He went from being Early-Church archenemy to Early-Church convert and catalyst for building and spreading the Church all over the world. He became a man who was to be persecuted, whipped, imprisoned, and stoned for protecting, proclaiming, and embodying the very thing he set out to destroy.

Talk about a turnaround!

If this is what God can do with a dangerous man like Saul, surely there is nothing impossible in our day for God!

One thing is for sure, as the Bible states unequivocally, God wants no one to perish!

> *The Lord is not slow in keeping his promise, as some understand slowness. Instead, he is patient with you, not wanting anyone to perish, but everyone to come to repentance.*

> (2 Peter 3:9, NIV)

So, the most important thing we can do as Christians staying faithful to the Word of God is to love all people, and believe in the power of God to save, remembering what Paul, himself said:

> *My message and my preaching were not with wise and persuasive words, but with a demonstration of the Spirit's power, so that your faith might not rest on human wisdom, but on God's power.*

> (1 Corinthians 2:4-5, NIV)

Reaching any community of individuals doesn't rely on our own wisdom or strength; it relies solely on the supernatural action and agency of the Holy Spirit. In fact, Jesus left us in no doubt of the essential ingredient to all salvation:

> *No one can come to me unless the Father who sent me draws them, and I will raise them up at the last day.*

> (John 6:44, NIV)

Nothing is impossible for God, but nothing is possible for us if we intend to do it without Him.

God can be in every conversation we have if we *let* Him; all that is needed for the Holy Spirit to be present is that we submit ourselves to Him and ensure that our lives and attitudes demonstrate the fruit of His Spirit (Galatians 5:22). In the case of talking with the LGBTQ+ community, this means that we consistently show love and respect to individuals and that we do not condemn them for their life choices but instead, point them to Jesus. It means that we speak with gentleness and with compassion always and let Jesus' Spirit draw them to Himself.

Furthermore, I believe we should be praying even more in our days. We have already considered in this book the changing and devastating shape of the world we live in... plagues, weather disasters, food shortages, climate change, wars etc. These things *will* happen, just as Jesus promised in Matthew 24, and the extra thing that Jesus mentioned, amongst these other calamities... that will also happen: '**many** will turn away from the faith' (Matthew 24:10, NIV, my emphasis added).

Not one of us wants to be listed amongst that final statistic, I am sure!

PUTTING IT INTO PRACTICE

So then, how can we share Jesus with the LGBTQ+ community?

I believe there are four key ingredients that we need to consider in dealing with this question with real integrity. Let's explore each one of them in more detail...

1. Love

I've written a lot about loving the LGBTQ+ community in this book but I can't overemphasise how important love is...

It's essential that we love all people, regardless of who they are and what life choices they make.

Jesus met many people whose lifestyle and life choices He didn't agree with, yet this did not change how He treated them. Always, He gave them His time, He showed warmth and hospitality, He was unworried by interruptions that might alter His agenda, and He was patient with them. He never once condoned sin, but He always loved the one who had fallen into sin.

We must never forget that Jesus stepped down into this world to save it.

Why?

Because God so **loved** the world! (John 3:16).

God loves individuals who identify themselves as part of the LGBTQ+ community, even if He doesn't affirm their choices. Never forget that His Son spread His arms wide on the cross and invited every single one of us to turn to Him through repentance, meaning a new way of life, so that we could all receive eternal life in relationship with Him. And that love holds no conditions whatsoever; sexuality issues can never and will never separate individuals from God's love (Romans 8).

Every conversation we have is an opportunity for the Holy Spirit to move.

A wise man once said to me, "our relationships are opportunities for conversations that lead to the cross." That means keeping the conversation line open; so, that also means not overreacting if you see a homosexual couple walk into church holding hands... Instead, the best counsel I can offer is this: pray for wisdom, then be kind and welcoming towards them. Later, speak to your church leaders in private and ask for their guidance.

As for church leaders, our role is to be very clear about where the Church stands and what the Bible says on this issue, but this must be done privately with the individuals in question and alongside the genuine commitment to journey with them as friends, regardless of their choices.

Something that I have witnessed recently is a number of local churches running really 'loving' courses on sexuality. Of course, this is commendable, and keeps love at the forefront of their teaching. However, there is a risk that courses like these may spend *too* much time emphasising love, yet never clarify where the Church stands on the issue of sexuality; never actually stating what the biblical record is. I think we owe it to everyone who comes to our churches to be very clear about clarifying the biblical record as early as possible and to do this with kindness and compassion. We need to be clear about what God's view on sexuality and holiness is, not cloud the issue by avoiding what may appear controversial or counter-cultural.

We need to keep love *and truth* in tandem!

We don't need to win wars with people – after all, aggression usually generates more aggression and what good is that? We need to hear the hearts of everyone whom we speak with, even if we do not agree personally with what they say or do, and we need to lovingly journey with them, praying that God will open hearts and minds to doing things His way.

Never forget, as I remarked in a previous chapter, the Bible says we are ministering to people who have been blinded:

The god of this age has blinded the minds of unbelievers,
so that they cannot see the light of the gospel that
displays the glory of Christ, who is the image of God.

(2 Corinthians 4:4, NIV)

The devil has blinded people so they cannot believe the gospel, so, of course, the world thinks the faithful Church has got it all wrong when it comes to LGBTQ+ and the decision to stand by the biblical record that anything outside of God's Genesis blueprint is sinful...

So, how will we ever help individuals understand? Well, that leads to the next essential ingredient, the Holy Spirit.

2. The Holy Spirit

When I started out in ministry at Reigate Baptist Church, I felt called to move nearer the church community. The problem standing before me was my wife... She loved her home half an hour away from the church and getting her to move was going to be an impossible task. Seriously, if you knew my wife, you'd know this to be true! So, I did what we all need to do, I handed it over to God.

One day, we were driving along when suddenly, Rachel said to me, "I sense God is telling me we should put my house up for sale in faith and move nearer the church."

I listened to her incredulous – clearly, God was on the case!

That same week we received a phone call from someone in the church who had left the area and wanted to offer us their house with a great discount. To keep a long story short, the person calling us had no idea we were looking, it was just divine timing. We bought the house just weeks before I took over as senior pastor in the church – a new home provided for us in the perfect location.

So often we fight our battles with our words when we should be fighting them with our prayers. God, by His Holy Spirit, opens hearts and eyes! We need to trust in Him! In fact, He wants us to rely on Him!

Reaching people with the gospel is no different. I once had a man come to see me in my office asking for help to commit his life to Jesus. He said, "I was ready on Sunday but I'm not doing it in front of everyone like all those others who tend to cry in public." I led him in a prayer of repentance, and despite himself, the tears flowed freely. Why? Because God touched Him by His Holy Spirit.

God has the key to unlock every single heart!

The Holy Spirit creates divine appointments, and He opens eyes and hearts. All we need to do is keep in step with the Spirit and He will do the rest.

When Elisha's servant came to him in a panic because the enemy army was coming to destroy them, the Bible records that something very exciting happened:

And Elisha prayed, "Open his eyes, LORD, so that he may see." Then the LORD opened the servant's eyes, and he looked and saw the hills full of horses and chariots of fire all around Elisha.

> *As the enemy came down toward him, Elisha prayed to the LORD, "Strike this army with blindness." So, he struck them with blindness, as Elisha had asked.*

(2 Kings 6:17-18, NIV)

Elisha prays – and God responds by opening his servant's eyes to see the Lord's army assembled and ready to win the battle.

Surely, this is of encouragement to us as believers in the battle we face against the demonic world. But it is also a reminder of how God can open the eyes of the spiritually blind so that they may see the true reality and see that God is at hand to save them.

Our LGBTQ+ brothers and sisters in the Church simply need us to welcome them, listen to them, and share with them the wonderful promise of Scripture: that there is life through faith in Jesus and repentance of our sins. That literally, 'where the spirit of the Lord is, there is freedom!' (2 Corinthians 3:17, NIV), and that that freedom comes by walking in God's ways!

The Bible also says that we need to collaborate with the Holy Spirit in restoration:

> *If someone is caught in a sin, you who live by the*
> *Spirit should restore that person gently. But watch*
> *yourselves... you also may be tempted.*

(Galatians 6:1, NIV)

Let's never forget that we are *all* susceptible to sinning, but we *all* have the responsibility before God to choose not to. We must never condemn others for their choices even if the Bible deems them to be sinful, but we must lovingly teach what the Bible says and pray that the Holy Spirit leads them to repentance.

To do this, we need to refrain from any judgmental attitudes. We need to be willing to enter into a longer-term friendship with each individual and not perceive anyone as needing a quick fix.

This is where discipleship comes in...

3. One-to-one discipleship

Discipleship is very much in line with what I have already said regarding choosing to love and spend time with people of all backgrounds.

However, I want to add one thing more that concerns me: There is an increasingly large movement of churches and Christians who seem to rely solely on 'one meal a week'. For them, the Sunday service is seen as equivalent to match day (humour me with this football metaphor) when, in fact, the real 'game' takes place in the home, in the workplace, in the schools, in the quiet place with God. I wonder if any of us have fallen into that trap?

If we have, we do not need to condemn ourselves but simply repent and adjust our attitudes and actions accordingly.

As believers, we can choose to live in prayer, in Scripture and in relationship with God through His Holy Spirit. At the same time, as others have remarked on past occasions, 'no man is an island' and Hebrews 10:25 tells us not to give up meeting *together* but to encourage one another.

This 'being together' factor is hugely important to our spiritual growth, and it is essential when witnessing to anyone, particularly the LGBTQ+ community.

It's all well and good telling a community of people that their lifestyle is not the way God intends, but is that going to be enough? Of course not! Every individual needs to be treated with kindness and given the gift of your time and commitment to lovingly explain as Jesus would have done; they need to understand if you are telling them the truth, why this is the case, and how they should live to please God.

There are no short, sharp solutions, however, and this cannot be carried out in one conversation only. No, all this can only take place if individuals are taken on a journey through the Word of God.

This is why one-to-one discipleship is key.

It is about going on the journey together.

One of my favourite Bible stories is the 'Emmaus Road', when Jesus appears to two of His disciples in the wake of His crucifixion and resurrection. They are clearly troubled at the turn of events as they had hoped Jesus would redeem Israel. Partaking in their conversation as the three of them journey along the road together, Jesus remarks:

> *"How foolish you are, and how slow to believe all that the prophets have spoken! Did not the Messiah have to suffer these things and then enter his glory?" And beginning with Moses and all the Prophets, he explained to them what was said in all the Scriptures concerning himself.*

(Luke 24:25-27, NIV)

Evidently, Jesus' disciples had a false understanding of what Scripture said would happen to Jesus in being crucified on a cross. They were confused, so, beginning with Moses and all the prophets, Jesus took them on a one-to-one discipleship tour of Scripture (granted, in this case, it was a ratio of 1:2 which works just as effectively). The point is, after His initial remark, Jesus was patient with them and allowed Scripture to speak for itself in revealing the truth in a way they could understand. Can you imagine what an incredible conversation that must have been!

Next, we see the most exciting prospect of all one-to-one discipleship... the point when the truth breaks in:

*When he was at the table with them, he took bread,
gave thanks, broke it and began to give it to them. Then
their eyes were opened, and they recognized him, and
he disappeared from their sight. They asked each other,
"Were not our hearts burning within us while he talked
with us on the road and opened the Scriptures to us?"*

(Luke 24:30-32, NIV)

The Holy Spirit brought revelation and opened their eyes! Do you see the power of one-to-one discipleship through the Scriptures? This is why it is so important to keep up relationship with all people of all walks of life including the LGBTQ+ community, because God can open the eyes of anyone and everyone!

We just have to be available and willing and walking in tune with the Spirit if we want God to consider using us as part of someone's journey.

And now, for the final key ingredient that propels us to act in line with God's will... prayer.

4. Prayer for revival

Finally, alongside all the above in building relationship with those within the LGBTQ+ community, we must be committed to praying for revival.

Let's not forget the increasing godlessness in the world around us, evidenced by the Tower of Babel-like spirit which is building a world where the people are literally as gods. This kind of world is one where God is being pushed out.

Out of education.

Out of politics.

Out of arts and media.

Out of business.

Out of the family.

Out of every single sphere of society in general... And where instead, the world is pushing ungodly agendas and people are being encouraged to be and do what the Bible would class as an abomination to God.

Is this not devastating?

Furthermore, did not God give the people over to their sinful desires in Romans 1, as we already highlighted? And are we not seeing history repeat itself *in our days* as God gives society over to our sinful desires?

What can be done to stop the world in its tracks?

Surely, it's all too big for us now – what can we do?

I believe there are only two answers to all that is going on in the world:

We need either a great move of God, or the return of Jesus Christ our King!

With the LGBTQ+ movement in full flow, it is very unlikely that anyone is going to hear what Christians have to say on the matter and suddenly change direction and choose to live a biblical lifestyle concerning sexuality. The only way anyone will choose a kingdom life over an earthly life is if they have a revelation from God of a kingdom *so great* and the opportunity for a relationship with a God *so wonderful* that they would do anything to grasp it. Just like the man who sold everything he had to gain the precious pearl... Will they give up everything for the sake of knowing Jesus?

Ultimately, the only way this is going to happen is if God intervenes as He has in the past.

Let me share a story with you to illustrate my point.

A friend of mine recently spoke about a retreat he was on to the Hebridean Islands. He described how the highlight for him was spending each evening sharing dinner with a group of Christians, one of whom was an elderly lady who had been involved in a revival in the Hebrides. Every evening, the group would ask this humble woman to tell them stories about what it was like when the revival broke out, and with every story recounted they sat in awe of the power of God.

On one occasion, they asked the lady how the revival started for her. She replied by telling them how, one evening, whilst relaxing inside her home with a friend, both of them heard a sudden scream. When they ran outside to see what was happening, they found her father on his knees in the front garden praying a prayer of repentance. He had been overcome by the Holy Spirit unexpectedly and had fallen to his knees by the realisation of the weight of his sin before God.

Can you imagine this happening today, in our times? In a time where the world seems to be kicking God out of every part of our world? In a time where so many are choosing to live in a way that is contrary to God's best revealed in the Bible and actively promoting a lifestyle that is completely offensive to God? Wouldn't it be AMAZING if suddenly, those who arrogantly push an agenda which goes against the Word of God, were to fall to their knees in repentance and start praising God!

It may sound impossible, but God has done it many times over the years – and there is no reason to think that He can't do it all over again. I love to hear about the Welsh revivals where people were going about their day-to-day business when God broke in. Tales of individuals working in the fields who found themselves unexpectedly overwhelmed by the Spirit of God to such an extent that they repented and were swamped by the love of God! Revivals where the pubs were emptied out and all-night prayer and praise took place instead!

Can you imagine how remarkable that must have been!

The world and its agendas may seem far from God, but the power of God has the ability to cut people to the heart as we see happening in Acts 2. Having heard the passionate and Spirit-inspired words of Peter explaining the gospel to them, the people were literally 'cut to the heart' and asked the question, 'what should we do?' (Acts 2:37, NIV). And what was Peter's concise response? 'Repent and be baptised' (v.38, NIV). The Bible says God is a God who does not change (Malachi 3:6) so why should things be any different for us today? The God who cut 3,000 individuals to the heart on that day of Pentecost is the same God today who can cut thousands more to the heart...

The question is are we willing *to pray* that He does exactly that?

For anyone reading about the revivals of the past, there is usually one of two reactions. Either they get excited, or they get sceptical. Personally, I get very excited because I once had a similarly powerful God encounter in my own life.

A group of us from our church had been to New Wine, a Christian festival held during the summer holiday. Sadly, we all had to leave early due to the sudden arrival of bad weather. So, some of the group decided to host a praise service at the church the day after we returned, to celebrate God and our time together as a group.

What happened in that time together, I will never forget.

For years I have been very jealous of those people who fall over in services; I'm not into any sense of 'charismatic mania' unless it is real, and over the years I have witnessed both the real and the questionable. That evening I had a very heavy spirit, I was not in a good place and, quite frankly, I didn't want to be there.

My wife Rachel decided to take the children home early, and I stayed on a little longer.

Then something unexpected happened.

We were praising God, singing songs whilst I sat on a chair in the main auditorium. As I sat there, I was quite surprised to notice one person from our group sitting next to me with a laptop watching the Manchester United game. I found this really strange and not quite right. I started to feel very critical inside, when all of a sudden, I began praying out in tongues, almost involuntarily. Then, unexpectedly, I fell face down and started wailing in a way that I have never wailed in my entire life. I was screaming out, yet inside I felt like I was being released from something; I almost felt as though I were a spectator of what was going on. On the one hand I was wailing; on the other, I was assessing the wailing with awe from the inside. It's quite impossible to explain, but I knew I was repenting either for myself, or for myself and others. It was simply strange!

Afterwards, I wondered whether what I experienced then was a taste of what is to come. That, in the future, perhaps this same scenario is going to happen to a lot of people, and I needed to experience it to understand it when it arrives and when I see it happening to others around me. I really don't know, but I know how real this experience was – and I am still seeking God's revelation as to why He allowed me to experience it.

The truth is, increasingly, the world and the worldwide Church are accepting some extremely ungodly practices and incorporating them into our societies and psyche without question. But, sooner or later, God is going to stop giving people over to their sin (as we explored in Romans 1), He is going to stop ignoring it for a time (Acts 17), and He is going to call everyone everywhere to repent (Acts 17).

I believe we are in need of and close to a move of God!

Repentance may seem like a dirty word both in and outside the Church, but it does not mean we can bury it under a so-called 'grace is enough' doctrine. We should be very concerned by the increasingly woolly way in which repentance and sinful behaviour are perceived and taught by the Church. I wonder, are we keeping to the biblical record or are we adapting it to 'itch the ears' of the culture around us (see 2 Timothy 4)?

I had a great and timely reminder of the seriousness and centrality of true repentance in God's plan recently, when I read an account of the Holy Spirit falling on Cane Ridge in the book, *God's Generals: The Revivalists*:

> *Two or three of my acquaintances from a distance were struck down. I sat patiently by one of them, whom I knew to be a careless sinner, for hours, and observed with critical attention everything that passed from the beginning to the end. I noticed the momentary reviving's as from death – the humble confession of sin – the fervent prayer, and the ultimate deliverance – then the solemn thanks and praise to God – the affectionate exhortation to companions and to the people around, to repent and come to Jesus. I was astonished at the knowledge of the gospel truth displayed in the address. The effect was, that several sunk down into the same appearance of death. After attending to many such cases, my conviction was complete that it was a good work - the work of God; nor*

*has my mind wavered since on the subject. Much did I then see,
and much have I since seen, that I considered to be fanaticism;
but this should not condemn the work. The Devil has always
tried to ape the works of God, to bring them into disrepute. But
that cannot be a satanic work, which brings men to humble
confession and forsaking sin - to solemn prayer – fervent
praise and thanksgiving, and to sincere and affectionate
exhortations to sinners to repent and go to Jesus the Saviour.*[57]

Does this not make your hairs stand on end?

That when a move of God happens, people fall under the
power of God and repent of evil?

It seems to me that, in contrast to what is experienced by
Cane Ridge, the focus of many churches is to make friends
with those listening at the expense of speaking truth – and
I do not consider our own church to be exempt from this. As
2 Timothy 4 states, a time will come when people will 'not
endure sound doctrine' but will actively look for truths that fit
with their agenda (NIV). This is a warning which I try to keep
at the forefront of my own preaching; I do not want to be one
such speaker who favours culture over what God is saying in
His God-breathed Word, the Bible. **No way!**

Ultimately, I believe that as church leaders and as believers,
we can choose to speak truth and love our neighbours
simultaneously. However, it is up to individuals whether they
accept and receive our words or reject them.

We can seek to be loving always in the way we convey our
message. However, we cannot downplay the truth as to what
is and isn't sinful; we must proclaim the gospel *as it is.*

We can't sell the kingdom of God to people like a new car
salesman, adding and removing the things that the buyer
prefers in order to lower the cost to get them to accept it.

Think about it: It's true that you can remove the wheels and engine to make the price more attractive, but this means the car won't get prospective buyers to their destination.

It's the same with truth.

If you sell the gospel but omit to explain how sin needs to be repented for at the cross of Jesus Christ, then it will never get an individual to the destination that God promises to all who sincerely repent... the wonder of heaven and incredible relationship with Him!

Therefore, as God's people, I want us to be unwavering and to really get this! We must tell *the real gospel*, we must pray for all people and love all people, and where the mission to reach them is impossible... pray for God to move - in the hearts of individuals and across the whole world!

SO, WHAT NOW AND WHAT NEXT?

In our time today, it is sadly obvious that the world is far from God.

The answer is Jesus.

The strategy is a move of the Holy Spirit.

Jesus demonstrated the best model for us to follow: Be available to all; speak the truth; collaborate with the Holy Spirit in laying hands on, healing and delivering people when He requires it; restore people by journeying with them in one-to-one discipleship; and encourage them to set their hearts on the kingdom to come rather than the fading kingdom in which we currently live.

It really is that simple.

Impossible without God.

More than possible... when we put Him and His Word at the centre!

It is time for the Church to stand on the Word of God, in the Spirit of God, lovingly but without compromise!

The question is, are we ready to answer the challenge?

Epilogue

Let me end by reiterating what I have said throughout this book... Truly, I have agonised over the topic of sexuality and holiness when it comes to LGBTQ+ and whether God affirms same-sex relationships according to the biblical record.

I would love to be able to close the issue down and state that the Bible says sexual relationships outside of one man and one woman are OK. But I must be honest: I have found no evidence within the Bible to support this view.

I do not write this book with a vitriolic demeanor nor is it my intention to malign and cause hurt to those who identify themselves with the LGBTQ+ community.

If anyone would interpret what I have written as an attempt at 'conversion therapy', a topic that has been so prevalent in the News since early 2022, I would be saddened because I wish to clarify that I take the same view expressed by the Evangelical Alliance when interviewed recently; that it is utterly right for the government in the United Kingdom to end coercive and abusive practices but equally, it is important that the government not infringe freedom of speech and thereby ensure that individuals can receive prayer and spiritual support regarding LGBTQ+ *if they elect to of their own free will.*[58]

I write from a place of sincere concern for how things will play out amongst the Church; as Christians worldwide come to terms with having to decide where they stand as individuals on the topic of LGBTQ+, and whether this will lead to them choosing to 'swap' churches in order to be part of one which suits their own theological convictions.

Personally, I will be very sad to see this happen if it arises out of a wish to affirm LGBTQ+ and deviate from God's biblical perspective on sexuality. But, I believe it *will* happen and in the not-too-distant future.

Such a phenomenon will also affect pastors, priests and ministers, who will have to decide whether they can continue to serve in certain churches as the various denominations vote on various LGBTQ+ decisions.

If that, is you, reader, whether you are for or against any changes, I want you to know that I feel your pain, and I pray that God will bring His revelation to us all and help us clarify *what His view is* when it comes to these significant issues.

That is why I'd like to end by sharing some advice which I think applies to everyone (including myself) in this difficult discussion; something I believe to be more important than getting our theological understanding right on this matter. That advice concerns *how we treat each other...*

I read recently a wonderful book called *Imagine Heaven*. It is a book containing true stories of many individuals over the years who all claim to have had a near death experience where they have encountered Jesus. There is one encounter among them that rocked me to the core... It was the encounter of a man called Steve Sjogren who worked himself to the bone, and one day, suddenly, died. According to his story, whilst no longer alive, he encountered God and God asked him a simple yet profound question:

"Do you know the names of your children's friends?"[59]

What a strange question for God to ask at such a time as death, yet how poignant!

I know we can never know if this man's story was true or fabricated, not until we get to heaven and ask the Lord Himself... But I believe this is the type of question our Lord *would* ask. It reminds me of something I wholeheartedly believe to be true because it echoes the model that Jesus gave us: God is not bothered about our success in life or even our biblical knowledge. What concerns Him most is how we have behaved towards others...

Have we acted as Jesus would have done?

Have we shown compassion?

Have we cared for the needs of others?

Have we taken time *to love other people well*?

As I ponder whether I have loved people well, I'm afraid I believe in many cases, I have fallen short.

Therefore, I want to close with the most important advice for all of us as Christians.

Regardless of whether we believe same-sex relationships are a sin or not...

Please, let's love one another.

Be kind and gracious to one another.

Not forgetting that surely it would be a greater sin to treat anyone adversely on account of their sexual orientation and practice.

Let me say it one more time.

Let's choose to love all people regardless...

And let's do it **by pointing all people to Jesus.**

It is possible to hold to truth and to love **in tandem**.

Notes

Introduction

1   Some denominations have already affirmed same-sex marriage:
    Sherwood H, (2021) 'Methodist Church to Allow Same-sex Marriage
    after 'Historic' Vote', www.theguardian.com last accessed: 12 April
    2022
    May C, (2016) 'United Reformed Church approves Gay Marriage
    Services', www.bbc.co.uk, last accessed: 2 May 2022
    The press association, (2016) 'Church of Scotland Votes to Allow
    Ministers to be in Same-sex Marriages', www.theguardian.com last
    accessed: 2 May 2022
    Wadhera C, (2021) 'Church in Wales Votes to Allow Blessings for
    Same-sex Marriages', www.independant.co.uk last accessed: 2 May
    2022

1. No right of reply

2   I have chosen to be discreet about the exact denomination and
    college with whom I trained, as I believe both mean well in their desire
    to propagate a loving attitude towards the LGBTQ+ community.
    This is a difficult subject for all concerned and it is important to
    acknowledge that the views held in a denomination and college will
    vary.

3. Validating the Bible; defining sin

3   Hailes S, *Premier Christianity Magazine*, 'Deconstructing Theology',
    (18 March 2019), pp. 58-67
4   Hailes S, *Premier Christianity Magazine*, 'Deconstructing Theology',
    pp. 58-67

5   Hailes S, *Premier Christianity Magazine*, 'Deconstructing Theology', pp. 58-67

6   Campolo B, in Hailes S, *Premier Christianity Magazine*, 'Deconstructing Theology', pp. 58-67

7   Zukeran P, (2019) 'The Historical Reliability of the Gospels', www.bible.org last accessed: 12 April 2022

8   Gerhard P, (no publication date) 'Why the Bible is Historically Reliable', www.revivalandreformation.org last accessed: 12 April 2022

9   Zukeran P, (2019) 'The Historical Reliability of the Gospels'

10 Kraby C, (no publication date) 'The Reliability of the Bible: 4 Quick Thoughts', www.reasonabletheology.org last accessed: 12 April 2022

11 Burrows M, *What Mean These Stones?* (New York: Meridian Books, 1956), p. 1

12 Wilson I, *The Bible is History*, (London: Weidenfeld & Nicolson, 1999), p. 221

13 Blomberg C L, *The Historical Reliability of the Gospels*, second edition, (Nottingham: Apollos, 2007), p. 327

14 Roberts M D, *Can We Trust the Gospels?* (Wheaton, Illinois: Crossway, 2007), p. 152

15 Reinsch W, (2018) 'Biblical Belshazzar Revealed', www.watchjerusalem.co.il last accessed: 12 April 2022,

16 Cohen J, (2013) '6 Things You May Not Know about The Dead Sea Scrolls' www.history.com last accessed 10 January 2022

17 Scholars speculate that the omission of Esther in the Dead Sea Scrolls may be due to the name of God never appearing in the book of Esther, making it therefore not a book that by Jewish tradition had to be preserved and buried. Other possibilities have been summarised by Dr Sidnie White Crawford in her article on the Book of Esther in the *Encyclopaedia of the Dead Sea Scrolls* (1: p. 269).

18 Cohen J, (2013) '6 Things You May Not Know about The Dead Sea Scrolls'

19 Cohen J, (2013) '6 Things You May Not Know about The Dead Sea Scrolls'

20 Begg A, *Brave by faith*, (Epsom: The Good Book Company, 2021), p. 34

21 Oakes J, (2009) 'What do the four parts of the of the statute in Nebuchadnezzar's dream represent?' www.evidenceforchristianity.org last accessed: 2 January 2022

22 Blanchard J, *The Complete Gathered Gold*, (Darlington: Evangelical Press, 2006), p. 595

4. A good thing the Law counts for nothing, right?

23 Vines M, *God and the Gay Christian*, (New York: Convergent Books, 2014), p. 78
24 Grenz S J, *Welcoming but not Affirming*, (Kentucky: John Knox Press, 1998), pp. 40-43
25 Grenz S J, *Welcoming but not Affirming*, (1998), pp. 40-43
26 Richardson J, *What God has made Clean*, (Baulkham Hills: MPA Books, 2003), pp. 8-11
27 Richardson J, *What God has made Clean*, (2003), pp. 8-11
28 Richardson J, *What God has made Clean*, (2003), pp. 8-11

5. Jesus had nothing to say on the issue, right?

29 Grenz S J, *Welcoming but not Affirming*, (1998), pp. 60-62
30 Grenz S J, *Welcoming but not Affirming*, (1998), pp. 60-62

6. Paul on same-sex relationships and signs of the times

31 Collins N and Coles G, (no publication date), 'Is same-sex attraction (or being gay) a sin?' centerforfaith.com last accessed: 16 November 2021
32 Grenz S J, *Welcoming but not Affirming*, (1998), pp. 48-49
33 Sprinkle P, (no publication date), 'Did adult consensual same-sex relationships exist in bible times?', centerforfaith.com last accessed: 16 November 2021
34 Sprinkle P, 'Did adult consensual same-sex relationships exist in bible times?'
35 Collins N and Coles G, 'Is same-sex attraction (or being gay) a sin?'

7. Fill the earth!

36 Standford Childrens Health (no publication date or author), 'Medical Genetics: How Chromosome Abnormalities Happen' last accessed 01 March 2022
37 Jacobson J, (2019), 'Is Sexual Orientation Genetic? Yes and No, an Extensive Study Finds', www.haaretz.com last accessed 1 March 2022

8. Not forgetting Sodom and Gomorrah

38 Janzen W, *Old Testament Ethics*, (Kentucky: Westminster/ John Knox Press, 1993), pp. 26-30
39 Janzen W, *Old Testament Ethics*, pp. 31-33
40 Via D O and Gagnon A J, *Homosexuality and the Bible*, (Minneapolis: Fortress Press, 2003), p. 5
41 DeYoung K, *What Does the Bible Really Teach about Homosexuality*, (Nottingham: IVP, 2015), p. 36
42 DeYoung K, *What Does the Bible Really Teach about Homosexuality*, p. 37

9. Kingdom over culture

43 Keller T, *The Way of Wisdom*, (London: Hodder & Stoughton, 2017), p. 317
44 Ligon G, *Bonhoeffer's the cost of Discipleship*, (Nashville, 1998), p. 99

10. A movement too far?

45 You can find out more on this by visiting www.stonewall.org.uk website and searching: *UK Workplace equality Index.*
46 Beal J, (12 March 2022) 'Parents revolt after American school Lessons on '64 genders', www.thetimes.co.uk last accessed 14 April 2022
47 Greenhalgh, H (20 May 2021) 'More Britons than ever before identify as lesbian, gay or bisexual', www.reuters.com last accessed: 15 November 2021
48 Lawrie E, (3 November 2021), 'Free speech row prof Kathleen Stock: Protests like anxiety dream', www.bbcnews.com last accessed: 16 November 2021
49 Bowcott O, (10 October 2018) 'UK Supreme Court backs bakery that refused to make a gay marriage cake', www.theguardian.com last accessed: 15 November 2021.
50 Thompson, David, (14 October 2021) 'Stonewalls influence on the BBC and Ofcom revealed', www.bbcnews.com last accessed: 15 October 2021
51 Adams R, (28 October 2021) 'Sussex Professor resigns after Transgender rights row', www.the guardian.com last accessed: 15 October 2021
52 Robertson D, (23 October 2020) 'Steve Chalke and the threat to prosecute evangelical churches', www.evangelicalfocus.com last accessed: 14 April 2022

11. Churches, the world and chastisement

53 Kendall R T, *We've Never Been This Way Before*, (Florida: Charisma house, 2020), p. 51
54 Kendall R T, *We've Never Been This Way Before*, pp. 49-58
55 'Stephen Fry on God – The Meaning of Life' with Byrne G, (1 February 2015) RTE One (online video and transcript) can be found at: www.youtube.com
56 Kendall R T, *We've Never Been This Way Before*, pp. 49-58

12. Sharing Jesus with the LGBTQ+ community

57 Liardon, R, *God's Generals: The Revivalists*, (Florida: Roberts Liardon Ministries, 2008), pp. 224-225

Epilogue

58 Webster D, (1 April 2022) 'Confusion over government conversion therapy plans', www.eauk.org last accessed: 9 May 2022
59 Burke J & K, *Imagine Heaven Devotional: 100 Reflections to Bring Heaven to Your Life Today* (Grand Rapids: Baker books: 2018), pp. 16-17

Printed in the United States
by Baker & Taylor Publisher Services